JOURNEY'S END

A Play in

by
R. C. SHERRIFF

SAMUEL FRENCH

FRENCH

LONDON
NEW YORK TORONTO SYDNEY HOLLYWOOD

JOURNEY'S END

First produced by the Incorporated Stage Society at the Apollo Theatre, London, W.C., December 9th, 1928, and subsequently at the Savoy Theatre, Strand, London, W.C., January 21st, 1929, with the following cast of characters—

(In the order of their appearance)

CAPTAIN HARDY	. . . . . . Reginald Smith
LIEUTENANT OSBORNE	. . . . . George Zucco
PRIVATE MASON	. . . . . . Alexander Field
LANCE-CORPORAL BROUGHTON	. . . . Richard Caldicott
2ND LIEUTENANT RALEIGH	. . . . Maurice Evans
CAPTAIN STANHOPE .	. . . . . Colin Clive
2ND LIEUTENANT TROTTER	. . . . Melville Cooper
2ND LIEUTENANT HIBBERT	. . . . Robert Speaight
THE COMPANY SERGEANT-MAJOR	. . . Tristan Rawson
THE COLONEL	. . . . H. G. Stoker
A GERMAN SOLDIER	. . . . . . Geoffrey Wincott

The Play produced by JAMES WHALE

SYNOPSIS OF SCENES

The Scene is laid in a Dug-out in the British trenches before St Quentin, March, 1918

The Curtain is lowered once during Act II and twice during Act III, to denote lapse of time.

ACT I

Evening on Monday, the 18th March, 1918

ACT II

SCENE I   Tuesday morning
SCENE II   Tuesday afternoon

ACT III

SCENE I   Wednesday afternoon
SCENE II   Wednesday night
SCENE III   Thursday, towards dawn

JOURNEY'S END

ACT I

SCENE—*A Dug-out in the British trenches before St Quentin.*
A few rough steps lead into the trench above, through a low doorway.
A table LC *occupies a good space of the dug-out floor. A wooden frame, covered with wire netting, stands against the left wall and serves the double purpose of a bed and a seat for the table. A wooden bench against the back wall makes another seat, and two boxes serve for the other sides.*
Another wire-covered bed is fixed in the right corner beyond the door-way.
Gloomy tunnels lead out of the dug-out to up L *and down* R.
Except for the table, beds, and seats, there is no furniture save the bottles holding the candles, and a few tattered magazine pictures pinned to the wall of girls in flimsy costumes.
The earth walls deaden the sounds of war, making them faint and far away, although the front line is only fifty yards ahead. The flames of the candles that burn day and night are steady in the still, damp air.
(See the Ground Plan of the Scene.)

The evening of a March day. A pale glimmer of moonlight shines down the narrow steps into one corner of the dug-out. Warm yellow candle-flames light the other corner from the necks of two bottles on the table. Through the doorway can be seen the misty grey parapet of a trench and a narrow strip of starlit sky. A bottle of whiskey, a jar of water, and a mug stand on the table amongst a litter of papers and magazines. An officer's equipment hangs in a jumbled mass from a nail in the wall.
During the Act the 'Verey' light comes on and off every minute. At the rise of the CURTAIN *there is a distant rumble of guns.*
CAPTAIN HARDY, *a red-faced, cheerful-looking man, with gas mask on, but no belt, is sitting on a box by the* R *of the table, intently drying a sock over a candle-flame. He wears a heavy trench-boot on his left leg, and his right foot, which is naked, is held above the damp floor by resting it on his left knee. His right boot stands on the floor beside him. As he carefully turns the sock this way and that—feeling it against his face to see if it is dry—he half sings, half hums a song—humming when he is not quite sure of the words, and marking time with the toes of his right foot.*

HARDY. 'One and Two, it's with Maud and Lou;
    Three and Four, two girls more;
    Five and Six, it's with—hm—hm—hm—
    Seven, Eight, Clara and Caroline——'

(He lapses into an indefinite humming, and finishes with a lively burst)

1

'Tick! Tock!—wind up the clock,
And we'll start the day over again.'

(*Machine-gun effect off* R)

LIEUTENANT OSBORNE'S *legs appear in the moonlit trench above,
and a tall, thin man comes slowly down the dug-out steps, stooping low
to avoid the roof. He takes his helmet off and reveals a fine head, with
close-cropped, iron-grey hair. He looks about 45—physically as hard as
nails*)

HARDY (*looking round*) Hullo, Osborne! Your fellows arriving?
(*Rubbing his foot*)
OSBORNE (*entering and hitching off his pack and dropping it in a
corner down* RC *by bed*) Yes. They're just coming in.
HARDY. Splendid! Have a drink.

(*Machine-gun effect*)

OSBORNE. Thanks. (*He crosses, passes behind the table and sits on the
bed* L)
HARDY (*passing the whiskey and a mug*) Use my mug if you like.
Don't have too much water. It's rather strong today.
OSBORNE (*slowly mixing a drink*) I wonder what it *is* they put in
the water.
HARDY. Some sort of disinfectant, I suppose.
OSBORNE. I'd rather have the microbes, wouldn't you?
HARDY. *I* would—yes——
OSBORNE. Well, cheero.
HARDY. Cheero. Excuse my sock, won't you?
OSBORNE. Certainly. It's a nice-looking sock.
HARDY. It is rather, isn't it? Guaranteed to keep the feet dry.
Trouble is, it gets so wet doing it.
OSBORNE. Stanhope asked me to come and take over. He's look-
ing after the relief coming in.
HARDY. Splendid! You know, I'm awfully glad you've come.
OSBORNE. I heard it was a quiet bit of line up here.
HARDY. Well, yes—in a *way*. But you never know. Sometimes
nothing happens for hours on end; then—all of a sudden—'over
she comes!'—rifle grenades—Minnies—and those bloody little
things like pineapples—you know.
OSBORNE. I know.
HARDY. Swish—swish—swish—swish—BANG!
OSBORNE. All right—all right—I know.
HARDY. They simply blew us to bits yesterday. Minnies—enor-
mous ones; about twenty. Three bang in the trench. I really *am*
glad you've come; I'm not simply being polite.
OSBORNE. Do much damage?
HARDY. Awful. A dug-out got blown up and came down in the
men's tea. Damned annoying.

Osborne (*lighting his pipe and smoking*) I know. There's nothing worse than dirt in your tea.

Hardy. By the way, you know the big German attack's expected any day now?

Osborne. It's been expected for the last month.

Hardy. Yes, but it's very near now; there's funny things happening over in the Boche country. I've been out listening at night when it's quiet. There's more transport than usual coming up—you can hear it rattling over the *pavé* all night; more trains in the distance—puffing up and going away again, one after another bringing up loads and loads of men——

Osborne. Yes. It's coming—pretty soon now.

Hardy. Are you here for six days?

Osborne. Yes.

Hardy. Then I should think you'll get it—right in the neck. (*He puts on his sock*)

Osborne. Well, you won't be far away. Come along, let's do this handing over. Where's the map?

Hardy. Here we are. (*He gropes among the papers on the table and finds a tattered map which is on the* c *box behind the table*) We hold about two hundred yards of front line. We've got a Lewis gun just here—and one here, in this little sap. Sentry posts where the crosses are——

Osborne. Where do the men sleep?

Hardy. *I* don't know. The sergeant-major sees to that. (*He points off to the* L) The servants and signallers sleep in there. Two officers in here, and three in there. (*He points to the* R *hand tunnel*) That is, if you've *got* five officers. (*He puts on his trench boot*)

Osborne. We've only got four at present, but a new man's coming up tonight. He arrived at transport lines a day or two ago.

Hardy. I hope you get better luck than I did with *my* last officer. He got lumbago the first night and went home. Now he's got a job lecturing young officers on 'Life in the Front Line'.

Osborne. Yes. They do send some funny people over here nowadays. I hope we're lucky and get a youngster straight from school. They're the kind that do best.

Hardy. I suppose they are, really. (*He sits up and lights a cigarette*)

Osborne. Five beds, you say? (*He examines the one he is sitting on*) Is this the best one?

Hardy. Oh, no. (*He points to the bed in the* R *corner*) *That's* mine over there. The ones in the other dug-out (*pointing to* R) haven't got any bottoms to them. You keep yourself in by hanging your arms and legs over the sides. Mustn't hang your legs too low, or the rats gnaw your boots.

Osborne. You got many rats here?

Hardy. I should say—roughly—about two million; but then, of course, I don't see them all. (*He begins to put on his sock and draw on his boot*) Well, there's nothing else you want to know, is there?

OSBORNE. You haven't told me anything yet.

HARDY. What else do you *want* to know?

OSBORNE. Well, what about trench stores?

HARDY. You *are* a fussy old man. Anybody'd think you were in the Army. (*He rises and goes behind the table, finds a tattered piece of paper, and shows it to Osborne*) Here you are: hundred and fifteen rifle grenades—I shouldn't use them if I were you; they upset Jerry and make him offensive. Besides, they are rusty, in any case. Then there's five hundred Mills bombs, thirty-four gum boots——

OSBORNE. That's seventeen pairs——

HARDY. Oh, no; twenty-five right leg and nine left leg. But everything's down here. (*He hands the list to Osborne and moves L of the table*)

OSBORNE. Did you check it when you took over?

HARDY. No. I think the Sergeant-Major did. It's quite all right.

OSBORNE. I expect Stanhope would like to see you before you go. He always likes a word with the company commander he's relieving.

HARDY. How *is* the dear young boy? Drinking like a fish, as usual? (*He sits at the table*)

OSBORNE. Why do you say that?

HARDY. Well, damn it, it's just the natural thing to ask about Stanhope. (*He pauses, and looks curiously at Osborne*) Poor old man. It must be pretty rotten for you, being his second in command, and you such a quiet, sober old thing.

OSBORNE. He's a long way the best company commander we've got.

HARDY. Oh, he's a good chap, I know. But I never *did* see a youngster put away the whiskey he does. D'you know, the last time we were out resting at Valennes he came to supper with us and drank a whole bottle in one hour fourteen minutes—we timed him.

OSBORNE. I suppose it amused everybody; I suppose everybody cheered him on, and said what a splendid achievement it was. '

HARDY. He didn't want any 'cheering' on——

OSBORNE. No, but everybody thought it was a big thing to do. (*There is a pause*) Didn't they?

HARDY. Well, you can't help, somehow, *admiring* a fellow who can do that—and then pick out his own hat all by himself and walk home——

OSBORNE. When a boy like Stanhope gets a reputation out here for drinking, he turns into a kind of freak show exhibit. People pay with a bottle of whiskey for the morbid curiosity of seeing him drink it.

HARDY. Well, naturally, you're biased. You have to put him to bed when he gets home.

OSBORNE. It rather reminds you of bear-baiting—or cock-fighting—to sit and watch a boy drink himself unconscious.

HARDY. Well, damn it, it's pretty dull without *something* to liven people up. I mean, after all—Stanhope really *is* a sort of freak; I mean it *is* jolly fascinating to see a fellow drink like he does—glass after glass. He didn't go home on his last leave, did he?

OSBORNE. No.

HARDY. I suppose he didn't think he was fit to meet papa. (*A pause*) You know his father's vicar of a country village?

OSBORNE. I know.

HARDY (*laughing*) Imagine Stanhope spending his leave in a country vicarage sipping tea! He spent his last leave in Paris, didn't he? (*He rises, moves* R *and looks at the picture on the wall*)

OSBORNE. Yes.

HARDY. I bet it was *some* leave! (*He sits again*)

OSBORNE. Do you know how long he's been out here?

HARDY. A good time, I know.

OSBORNE. Nearly three years. He came out straight from school —when he was eighteen. He's commanded this company for a year—in and out of the front line. He's never had a rest. Other men come over here and go home again ill, and young Stanhope goes on sticking it, month in, month out.

HARDY. Oh, I know he's a jolly good fellow——

OSBORNE. I've seen him on his back all day with trench fever— then on duty all night——

HARDY. Oh, I know; he's a splendid chap!

OSBORNE. And because he's stuck it till his nerves have got battered to bits, he's called a drunkard.

HARDY. Not a drunkard; just a—just a hard drinker; but you're quite right about his nerves. They *are* all to blazes. (*He leans his elbow on the table to enjoy the story*) Last time out resting we were playing bridge and something happened—I don't remember what it was; some silly little argument—and all of a sudden he jumped up and knocked all the glasses off the table! Lost control of himself; and then he—sort of—came to—and cried——

OSBORNE. Yes, I know.

HARDY. You heard about it?

OSBORNE. He told me.

HARDY. Did he? We tried to hush it up. It just shows the state he's in. (*He rises, goes up* R, *and puts on his pack. Glasses first, webbing equipment next. There is a pause*) You know, Osborne, *you* ought to be commanding this company.

OSBORNE. Rats!

HARDY. Of course you ought. It sticks out a mile. I know he's got pluck and all that, but, damn it, man, you're twice his age— and think what a dear, level-headed old thing you are.

OSBORNE. He was out here before I joined up. His experience alone makes him worth a dozen people like me.

HARDY. You know as well as I do, you ought to be in command.

Osborne. There isn't a man to touch him as a commander of men. He'll command the battalion one day if——
Hardy. Yes, if! (*He laughs*)
Osborne. You don't know him as I do; I love that fellow. I'd go to hell with him.
Hardy. Oh, you sweet, sentimental old darling!
Osborne. Come along. Finish handing over and stop blithering.
Hardy. There's nothing else to do.
Osborne. What about the log-book?
Hardy. God! you are a worker. Oh, well. Here we are. (*He crosses to* l, *finds a tattered little book and throws it on the table above Osborne*) Written right up to date in my own fairy handwriting: '5 p.m. to 8 p.m. All quiet. German airman flew over trenches. Shot a rat.'
Osborne. Did he?
Hardy. No, I shot the rat, you ass. Well, finish up your whiskey. I want to pack my mug. I'll leave you that drop in the bottle.
Osborne. Thanks. (*He drinks up his whiskey and hands Hardy the mug*)
Hardy (*crossing* r *of the table*) I'll be off. (*He wipes the mug with a dirty rag and hooks it on his belt, then gets the stick and tin hat off the bed* r)
Osborne. Aren't you going to wait and see Stanhope?
Hardy. Well, no, I don't specially want to see him. He's so fussy about the trenches. I expect they *are* rather dirty. He'll talk for hours if he catches me. (*He hitches his pack over his shoulders, hangs on his gas satchel, map-case, binoculars, compass-case, until he looks like a travelling pedlar. As he dresses*) Well, I hope you have a nice six days. Don't forget to change your clothes if you get wet.
Osborne. No, papa.
Hardy. And don't forget about the big attack.
Osborne. Oh, Lord, no, I mustn't miss that; I'll make a note in my diary.
Hardy (*fully dressed*) There we are! Do I look every inch a soldier? (*He poses as Greek*)
Osborne. Yes. I should get quite a fright if I were a German and met you coming round a corner.
Hardy. I should bloody well hope you would. (*He goes up to the door of the dug-out*)
Osborne. Shouldn't be able to run away for laughing.
Hardy. Now don't be rude.

(*Machine-gun fires*)

(*He comes back to the table and leans over to light a cigarette from a candle, and looks down on the table*) Well, I'm damned. Still at it!
Osborne. What is?

HARDY. Why, that earwig. It's been running round and round
that candle since tea-time; must have done a mile.

OSBORNE. I shouldn't hang about here if I were an earwig.

HARDY. Nor should I. I'd go home. Ever had earwig races?

OSBORNE. No.

HARDY. Great fun. We've had 'em every evening.

OSBORNE. What are the rules?

HARDY. Oh, you each have an earwig, and start 'em in a line.
On the word 'Go' you dig your earwig in the ribs and steer him
with a match across the table. I won ten francs last night—had a
splendid earwig. You'll find him about here somewhere. I'll give
you a tip.

OSBORNE. Yes?

HARDY. Promise not to let it go any further?

OSBORNE. Yes.

HARDY. Well, if you want to get the best pace out of an earwig,
dip it in whiskey—makes 'em go like hell!

OSBORNE. Right. Thanks awfully.

HARDY. Well, I must be off. Cheero!

OSBORNE. Cheero!

(HARDY *goes up the narrow steps into the trench above, singing
softly and happily to himself*)

'One and Two, it's with Maud and Lou;
Three and Four, two girls more——'

(*The words trail away into the night.*

OSBORNE *rises and gets his pack, which he had put down on
entrance, and puts it on the bed* R. *While he undoes it* MASON, *a
Soldier Servant, enters out of the tunnel from up* L *with two newspapers
under his arm and lays the table for supper*)

MASON. Excuse me, sir. Can I lay supper?

OSBORNE. Yes, do. (*He crosses, shuffles up the papers from the table
and puts them on the bed*)

MASON. Thank you, sir. (*He lays the table*)

OSBORNE (*moving back to* RC) What are you going to tempt us
with tonight, Mason?

MASON. Soup, sir—cutlets—and pineapple.

OSBORNE (*suspiciously*) Cutlets?

MASON. Well, sir—well, yes, sir—cutlets.

OSBORNE. What sort of cutlets?

MASON. Now, sir, you've got me. I shouldn't like to commit
meself too deep, sir.

OSBORNE. Ordinary ration meat? (*He sits on a box behind the table*)

MASON (*on his* L) Yes, sir. Ordinary ration meat, but a noo
shape, sir. Smells like liver, sir, but it 'asn't got that smooth, wet
look what liver's got.

(MASON *exits* L.

OSBORNE *sits up to the table and examines the map; after a slight pause, voices come from the trench above;* LANCE-CORPORAL BROUGHTON *appears at the top of the dug-out, and in a gruff voice says:* 'This is "C" Company 'Eadquarters, sir.'
A boyish voice replies: 'Oh, thanks.'
There is a pause, then the gruff voice says: 'Better go down, sir.'
The boyish voice replies: 'Right—thanks')

(*When* RALEIGH *enters,* BROUGHTON *exits.*
RALEIGH *comes groping down the steps and moves to* C. *Watching Osborne and standing to attention in the candle-light. He looks round, a little bewildered. He is a well-built, healthy-looking boy of about* 18 *with the very new uniform of a 2nd lieutenant.*
OSBORNE *looks up from the trench map, surprised and interested to see a stranger*)

OSBORNE. Hullo!
RALEIGH. Good evening (*he notices Osborne's grey hair and adds*), sir. (*He takes off his tin hat*)
OSBORNE. You the new officer?
RALEIGH. Er—yes, I've been to Battalion Headquarters. They told me to report here.
OSBORNE. Good. We've been expecting you. Sit down, won't you?
RALEIGH (*nervously*) Thanks. (*He sits gingerly on the box at the table opposite Osborne, with his pack on*)
OSBORNE. I should take your pack off.
RALEIGH. Oh, right. (*He rises and slips his pack from his shoulders, putting his tin hat and stick on the bed* R. *He has a belt on, no strap, then sits again*)
OSBORNE. Will you have a drink?
RALEIGH. Er—well——
OSBORNE. You don't drink whiskey?
RALEIGH (*hastily*) Oh, yes—er—just a small one, sir.
OSBORNE (*pouring out a small whiskey and adding water*) Whiskey takes away the taste of the water——
RALEIGH. Oh, yes? (*He pauses, and laughs nervously*)
OSBORNE. And the water takes away the taste of the whiskey. (*He hands Raleigh the drink. There is a pause*) Just out from England?
RALEIGH. Yes, I landed a week ago.
OSBORNE. Boulogne?
RALEIGH. Yes. (*A pause, then he self-consciously holds up his drink*) Well, here's luck, sir.

(*A Soldier walks across the back of the trench at this moment*)

OSBORNE (*taking a drink himself*) Good luck. (*He takes up a tin of cigarettes*) Cigarette? (*He hands Raleigh the tin*)
RALEIGH. Thanks.

OSBORNE (*holding a bottle across so that Raleigh can light his cigarette from the candle in it*) Ever been up in the line before? (*He helps himself*)

RALEIGH. Oh, no. You see, I only left school at the end of last summer term.

OSBORNE. I expect you find it a bit strange.

RALEIGH (*laughing*) Yes—I do—a bit——

OSBORNE. My name's Osborne. I'm second in command of the company. You only call me 'sir' in front of the men.

RALEIGH. I see. Thanks.

OSBORNE. You'll find the other officers call me 'Uncle'.

RALEIGH. Oh, yes? (*He smiles*)

OSBORNE. What's *your* name?

RALEIGH. Raleigh.

OSBORNE. I knew a Raleigh. A master at Rugby.

RALEIGH. Oh? He may be a relation. I don't know. I've got lots of uncles and—and things like that.

OSBORNE. We've only just moved into these trenches. Captain Stanhope commands the company.

RALEIGH (*suddenly brightening up*) I know. It's a frightful bit of luck.

OSBORNE. Why? D'you know him?

RALEIGH. Yes, rather! We were at school together—at least —of course—I was only a kid and he was one of the big fellows; he's three years older than I am.

(*There is a pause; Osborne seems to be waiting for Raleigh to go on, then suddenly he says:*)

OSBORNE. He's up in the front line at present, looking after the relief. (*Another pause*) He's a splendid chap.

RALEIGH. *Isn't* he? He was skipper of Rugger at Barford, and kept wicket for the eleven. A jolly good bat, too.

OSBORNE. Did you play Rugger—and cricket?

RALEIGH. Oh, yes. Of course, I wasn't in the same class as Dennis—I say, I suppose I ought to call him Captain Stanhope?

OSBORNE. Just 'Stanhope'.

RALEIGH. I see. Thanks.

OSBORNE. Did you get your colours?

RALEIGH. I did for Rugger. Not cricket.

OSBORNE. Rugger and cricket seem a long way from here.

RALEIGH (*laughing*) They do, rather.

OSBORNE. We play a bit of soccer when we're out of the line.

RALEIGH. Good!

OSBORNE (*thoughtfully*) So you were at school with Stanhope. (*Pause*) I wonder if he'll remember you? I expect you've grown in the last three years.

RALEIGH. Oh, I think he'll remember me. (*He stops, and goes on rather awkwardly*) You see, it wasn't only that we were just at school together; our fathers were friends, and Dennis used to come and stay with us in the holidays. Of course, at school I didn't see much of him, but in the holidays we were terrific pals.

OSBORNE. He's a fine company commander.

RALEIGH. I bet he is. Last time he was on leave he came down to the school; he'd just got his M.C. and been made a captain. It—sort of—made me feel——

OSBORNE. —keen?

RALEIGH. Yes. Keen to get out here. I was frightfully keen to get into Dennis's regiment. I thought, perhaps, with a bit of luck I might get to the same battalion.

OSBORNE. It's a big fluke to have got to the same company.

RALEIGH. I know. It's an amazing bit of luck. When I was at the base I did an awful thing. You see, my uncle's at the base— he has to detail officers to regiments——

OSBORNE. General Raleigh?

RALEIGH. Yes. I went to see him on the quiet and asked him if he could get me into this battalion. He bit my head off, and said I'd got to be treated like everybody else——

OSBORNE. Yes?

RALEIGH. —and next day I was told I *was* coming to this battalion. Funny, wasn't it?

OSBORNE. Extraordinary coincidence!

RALEIGH. And when I got to Battalion Headquarters, and the Colonel told me to report to 'C' Company, I could have cheered. I expect Dennis'll be frightfully surprised to see me. I've got a message for him.

OSBORNE. From the Colonel?

RALEIGH. No. From my sister.

OSBORNE. Your sister?

RALEIGH. Yes. You see, Dennis used to stay with us, and natur-ally my sister *(he hesitates)*—well—perhaps I ought not——

OSBORNE. That's all right. I didn't actually know that Stan-hope——

RALEIGH. They're not—er—officially engaged——

OSBORNE. No?

RALEIGH. She'll be awfully glad I'm with him here; I can write and tell her all about him. He doesn't say much in his letters; can we write often?

OSBORNE. Oh, yes. Letters are collected every day.

(There is a pause. The rumble of guns is more distinct)

RALEIGH. I see, thanks! *(He takes a drink)* You don't think Dennis'll mind my—sort of—forcing myself into his company? I never thought of that; I was so keen.

OSBORNE. No, of course he won't. *(Pause)* You say it's—it's a good time since you last saw him?

RALEIGH. Let's see. It was in the summer last year—nearly a year ago.

Osborne. You know, Raleigh, you mustn't expect to find him
—quite the same.

Raleigh. Oh?

Osborne. You see, he's been out here a long time. It—it tells
on a man—rather badly——

Raleigh (*thinking*) Yes, of course, I suppose it does.

Osborne. You may find he's—he's a little bit quick-tempered.

Raleigh (*laughing*) Oh, I know old Dennis's temper! I remember once at school he caught some chaps in a study with a bottle
of whiskey. Lord! the roof nearly blew off. He gave them a dozen
each with a cricket-stump.

(Osborne *laughs*)

He was so keen on the fellows in the house keeping fit. He was
frightfully down on smoking—and that sort of thing.

Osborne. You must remember he's commanded this company
for a long time—through all sorts of rotten times. It's—it's a big
strain on a man.

Raleigh. Oh, it must be.

Osborne. If you notice a—difference in Stanhope—you'll know
it's only the strain——

Raleigh. Oh, yes.

(Osborne *rouses himself and speaks briskly*)

Osborne. Now, let's see. (*He rises at the table and points to them*)
We've got five beds here—one each. Two in here and three in
that dug-out there. I'm afraid you'll have to wait until the others
come and pick the beds they want.

Raleigh. Righto!

Osborne. Have you got a blanket?

Raleigh. Yes, in my pack. (*He rises to get it*)

Osborne. Better wait and unpack when you know where you
are sleeping.

Raleigh. Righto! (*He sits down again* R *of the table*)

Osborne. We never undress when we're in the line. You can
take your boots off now and then in the daytime, but it's better to
keep pretty well dressed always.

Raleigh. I see. Thanks.

Osborne. I expect we shall each do about three hours on duty
at a time and then six off. We all go on duty at stand-to. That's
at dawn and dusk.

Raleigh. Yes.

(*The rumble of guns dies away*)

Osborne. I expect Stanhope'll send you on duty with one of us
at first—till you get used to it.

(*There is a pause.* Raleigh *turns on his seat and looks curiously up
the steps to outside and listens*)

RALEIGH. Are we in the front line here?

OSBORNE. No. That's the support line outside. The front line's about fifty yards farther on.

RALEIGH. How frightfully quiet it is!

OSBORNE. It's often quiet—like this.

RALEIGH. I thought there would be an awful row here—all the time.

OSBORNE. Most people think that.

(*Pause*)

RALEIGH. I've never known anything so quiet as those trenches we came by; just now and then I heard rifle firing, like the range at Bisley, and a sort of rumble in the distance.

(*The guns are heard rumbling again*)

OSBORNE. Those are the guns up north—up Wipers way. The guns are always going up there; it's never quiet like this. (*Pause*) I expect it's all very strange to you?

RALEIGH. It's—it's not exactly what I thought. It's just this—this quiet that seems so funny.

OSBORNE. A hundred yards from here the Germans are sitting in *their* dug-outs, thinking how quiet it is.

RALEIGH. Are they as near as that?

OSBORNE. About a hundred yards.

RALEIGH. It seems—uncanny. It makes me feel we're—we're all just waiting for something.

OSBORNE. We are, generally, just waiting for something. When anything happens, it happens quickly. Then we just start waiting again.

RALEIGH. I never thought it was like that.

OSBORNE. You thought it was fighting all the time?

RALEIGH (*laughing*) Well, yes, in a way.

OSBORNE (*after puffing at his pipe in silence for a while*) Did you come up by trench tonight—or over the top?

RALEIGH. By trench. An amazing trench—turning and twisting for miles, over a sort of plain.

OSBORNE. Lancer's Alley, it's called.

RALEIGH. Is it? It's funny the way it begins—in that ruined village, a few steps down into the cellar of a house—then right under the house and through a little garden—and then under the garden wall—then alongside an enormous ruined factory place—then miles and miles of plains, with those green lights bobbing up and down ahead—all along the front as far as you can see.

OSBORNE. Those are the 'Verey' lights. Both sides fire them over No-Man's Land—to watch for raids and patrols.

RALEIGH. I knew they fired lights. (*Pause*) I didn't expect so many—and to see them so far away.

OSBORNE. I know. (*He puffs at his pipe*) There's something rather romantic about it all.

RALEIGH (*eagerly*) Yes. I thought that, too.

OSBORNE. You must always think of it like that if you can. Think of it all as—as romantic. It helps.

(MASON *comes in with more dinner utensils*)

MASON. D'you expect the captain soon, sir? the soup's 'ot.

OSBORNE. He ought to be here very soon now. This is Mr Raleigh, Mason.

MASON. Good evening, sir.

RALEIGH. Good evening.

MASON (*to Osborne on his* L, *behind the table*) I've 'ad rather a unpleasant surprise, sir.

OSBORNE. What's happened?

MASON. You know that tin o' pineapple chunks I got, sir?

OSBORNE. Yes?

MASON. Well, sir, I'm sorry to say it's apricots.

OSBORNE. Good heavens! It must have given you a turn.

MASON. I distinctly said 'Pineapple chunks' at the canteen.

OSBORNE. Wasn't there a label on the tin?

MASON. No, sir. I pointed that out to the man. I said was 'e *certain* it was pineapple chunks?

OSBORNE. I suppose he said he was.

MASON. Yes, sir. 'E said a leopard can't change its spots, sir.

OSBORNE. What have leopards got to do with pineapple?

MASON. That's just what *I* thought, sir. Made me *think* there was something fishy about it. You see, sir, I know the Captain can't stand the sight of apricots. 'E said next time we 'ad them 'e'd wring my neck.

OSBORNE. Haven't you anything else?

MASON. There's a pink blancmange I've made, sir. But it ain't anywhere near stiff yet.

OSBORNE. Never mind. We must have the apricots and chance it.

MASON. Only I thought I'd tell *you*, sir, so as the captain wouldn't blame me.

OSBORNE (*looking at him*) All right, Mason.

(*Voices are heard in the trench above*)

That sounds like the captain coming now.

(*They both rise*)

MASON (*hastening away*) I'll go and dish out the soup, sir.

(*The voices grow nearer; two figures appear in the trench above and grope down the steps—the leading figure tall and thin, the other short and fat. The tall figure is* CAPTAIN STANHOPE, *who enters with trench coat, gas mask, tin hat and pack. At the bottom of the steps he straightens himself, pulls off his pack, and drops it on the floor up* C. RALEIGH *has risen and stands to attention over* R. TROTTER *puts his kit down on the up stage end of the* R *bed.* OSBORNE *is standing* C *by the table. Then* STANHOPE *takes off his helmet and throws it on the* R *hand bed. Despite his stars of rank he is no more than a boy; tall, slimly built, but broad-shouldered. His dark hair is carefully brushed; his uniform, though old and war-stained, is well cut and cared for. He is good-looking, rather from attractive features than the healthy good looks of Raleigh. Although tanned by months in the open air, there is a pallor under his skin and dark shadows under his eyes. His short and fat companion—2nd Lieutenant Trotter—is middle-aged and homely looking. His face is red, fat, and round; apparently he has put on weight during his war service, for his tunic appears to be on the verge of bursting at the waist. He carries an extra pack belonging to the officer left on duty in the line)*

STANHOPE (*as he takes off his pack, gas satchel, and belt*) Has Hardy gone?

OSBORNE. Yes. He cleared off a few minutes ago.

STANHOPE. Lucky for him he did. I had a few words to say to Master Hardy. You never saw the blasted mess those fellows left the trenches in. Dug-outs smell like cess-pits; rusty bombs; damp rifle grenades; it's perfectly foul. Where are the servants?

OSBORNE. In there.

STANHOPE (*calling into Mason's dug-out*) Hi! Mason!

MASON (*outside up* L) Coming, sir! Just bringing the soup, sir.

STANHOPE (*taking a cigarette from his case as he crosses and lighting it by the candle* L *of the table*) Damn the soup! Bring some whiskey!

OSBORNE. Here's a new officer, Stanhope—just arrived.

(RALEIGH *comes forward with outstretched hand.* STANHOPE *times his turn to meet Raleigh face to face*)

STANHOPE. Oh, sorry. (*He turns. Raleigh stands smiling awkwardly*) I didn't see you in this miserable light. (*He stops short at the sight of Raleigh. There is silence*)

RALEIGH. Hullo, Stanhope!

(STANHOPE *stares at Raleigh as though dazed.* RALEIGH *takes a step forward, half raises his hand, then lets it drop to his side*)

STANHOPE (*in a low voice*) How did you—get here?

RALEIGH. I was told to report to your company, Stanhope.

STANHOPE. Oh, I see. Rather a coincidence.

RALEIGH (*with a nervous laugh*) Yes.

(*There is a silence for a moment, broken by* OSBORNE *in a matter-of-fact voice*)

OSBORNE. I say, Stanhope, it's a terrible business. We thought we'd got a tin of pineapple chunks; it turns out to be apricots.

TROTTER. Ha! Give me apricots every time! I 'ate pineapple chunks; too bloomin' sickly for me!

RALEIGH. I'm awfully glad I got to your company, Stanhope.

STANHOPE. When did you get here?

RALEIGH. Well, I've only just come.

OSBORNE. He came up with the transport while you were taking over.

STANHOPE. I see.

(MASON *brings in a bottle of whiskey, a mug, and two plates of soup —so precariously that* OSBORNE *has to help with the soup plates on to the table*)

STANHOPE (*with sudden forced gaiety*) Come along, Uncle! Come and sit here. (*Then waving his hand towards the box on the* R *of the table*) You better sit there, Raleigh.

RALEIGH. Right!

(RALEIGH *sits awkwardly* R *of the table.* TROTTER *comes forward to Raleigh.* STANHOPE *sits at* C *of the table facing audience.* OSBORNE *over* L, *using bed as seat*)

TROTTER (*taking a pair of pince-nez from his tunic pocket, putting them on, and looking curiously at Raleigh*) You Raleigh?

RALEIGH. Yes.

(*Pause*)

TROTTER. I'm Trotter.

RALEIGH. Oh, yes?

(*Pause*)

TROTTER. How *are* you?

(*He shakes hands with Raleigh*)

RALEIGH. Oh, all right, thanks.

TROTTER. Been out 'ere before?

RALEIGH. No.

TROTTER. Feel a bit odd, I s'pose?

RALEIGH. Yes. A bit.

TROTTER (*getting a box to sit on*) Oh, well, you'll soon get used to it; you'll feel you've been 'ere a year in about an hour's time. (*He puts the box on its side and sits on it. It is too low for the table, and he puts it on its end. It is then too high. He tries the other side, which is too low; he finally contrives to make himself comfortable by sitting on his pack, placed on the side of the box*)

(MASON'S *entrance with two more plates of soup is when* TROTTER *goes to get pack from bed*)

OSBORNE. What kind of soup is this, Mason?

MASON. It's yellow soup, sir. (*Standing at attention* C)

OSBORNE. It's got a very deep yellow flavour.

TROTTER (*taking a melodious sip*) It wants some pepper; bring some pepper, Mason.

MASON (*anxiously*) I'm very sorry, sir. When the mess box was packed the pepper was omitted, sir.

TROTTER (*throwing his spoon with a clatter into the plate*) Oh, I say, but damn it!

(MASON *stands* L *of Stanhope, behind the table*)

OSBORNE. We must have pepper. It's a disinfectant.

TROTTER. You must have pepper in soup!

STANHOPE (*quietly*) Why wasn't it packed, Mason?

MASON. It—it was missed, sir.

STANHOPE. Why?

MASON (*miserably*) Well, sir, I left it to——

STANHOPE. Then I advise you never to leave it to anyone else again—unless you want to rejoin your platoon out there. (*He points into the moonlit trench*)

MASON. I'm—I'm very sorry, sir.

STANHOPE. Send one of the signallers.

MASON. Yes, sir.

(*He hastens to the tunnel entrance and calls*)

Bert, you're wanted!

(*A* SOLDIER *enters from up* L *with a rifle. He stands stiffly to attention* LC, R *of Stanhope*)

STANHOPE. Do you know 'A' Company Headquarters?

SOLDIER. Yes, sir.

STANHOPE. Go there at once and ask Captain Willis, with my compliments, if he can lend me a little pepper.

SOLDIER. Very good, sir.

(*He does not salute, slings rifle over shoulder, turns smartly and goes up the steps,* MASON *stopping him for a moment at the bottom of the steps to say confidently:* 'A screw of pepper, you ask for.' MASON *exits* L)

OSBORNE. We must have pepper.

TROTTER. I mean—after all—war's bad enough *with* pepper— (*noisy sip*) but war without pepper—it's—it's bloody awful!

OSBORNE. What's it like outside?

TROTTER. Quiet as an empty 'ouse. There's a nasty noise going on up north.

OSBORNE. Wipers, I expect. I believe there's trouble up there. I wish we knew more of what's going on.

TROTTER. So do I. Still, my wife reads the papers every morning and writes and tells me the news.

OSBORNE. Hardy says they had a lively time here yesterday. Three big Minnies right in the trench.

TROTTER. I know. And they left the bloomin' 'oles for us to fill in.

(MASON *arrives with cutlets in a frying pan, leaning over the table, serving from behind*)

What's this?

MASON. Meat, sir.

TROTTER. I know that. What sort?

MASON. Sort of cutlet, sir.

TROTTER. Sort of cutlet, is it? You know, Mason, there's cutlets and cutlets.

MASON. I know, sir; that one's a cutlet.

TROTTER. Well, it won't let me cut it.

MASON. No, sir?

TROTTER. That's a joke.

MASON. Oh! Right, sir. (*He goes out*)

OSBORNE (*studying the map*) There's a sort of ruin marked on this map—just in front of here, in No-Man's Land—called Beauvais Farm.

TROTTER. That's what we saw sticking up, skipper. I wondered what it was.

STANHOPE. Better go out and look at it tonight.

TROTTER. I expect a nasty German'll 'op out of it and say, 'Ock der Kaiser.' I 'ate ruins in No-Man's Land.

OSBORNE. There's only about sixty yards of No-Man's Land, according to this map—narrower on the left, from the head of this sap; only about fifty.

TROTTER (*who has been looking curiously at Stanhope, eating his meal with lowered head*) Cheer up, skipper. You *do* look glum!

STANHOPE. I'm tired.

OSBORNE. I should turn in and get some sleep after supper.

STANHOPE. I've got hours of work before I sleep.

OSBORNE. I'll do the duty roll and see the sergeant-major—and all that.

STANHOPE. That's all right, Uncle. I'll see to it. (*He turns to Raleigh for the first time*) Trotter goes on duty directly he's had supper. You better go with him—to learn.

RALEIGH. Oh, right.

TROTTER. Look 'ere, skipper, it's nearly eight now;

(*Grenades are fired off* R)

couldn't you make it 'alf-past?

STANHOPE. No. I told Hibbert he'd be relieved at eight. Will you take from eleven till two, Uncle?

OSBORNE. Right.

STANHOPE. Hibbert can do from two till four, and I'll go on from then till stand-to. That'll be at six.

(*Two whines and two shells*)

TROTTER. Well, boys! 'Ere we are for six days again. Six bloomin' eternal days. (*He makes a calculation on the table*) That's a hundred and forty-four hours; eight thousand six 'undred and forty minutes. *That* doesn't sound so bad; we've done twenty of 'em already. I've got an idea! I'm going to draw a hundred and forty-four little circles on a bit o' paper, and every hour I'm going to black one in; that'll make the time go all right.

STANHOPE. It's five to eight now. You better go and relieve Hibbert. Then you can come back at eleven o'clock and black in three of your bloody little circles.

TROTTER. I 'aven't 'ad my apricots yet!

STANHOPE. We'll keep your apricots till you come back.

TROTTER. I never knew anything like a war for upsetting meals. I'm always down for dooty in the middle of one.

STANHOPE. That's because you never stop eating.

TROTTER. Any'ow, let's 'ave some coffee. Hi! Mason! Coffee!

MASON. Coming, sir!

TROTTER (*rises, so does* RALEIGH. TROTTER *goes up* RC *and gets his kit on.* RALEIGH *does likewise over* R) Well, I'll get dressed. Come on, Raleigh.

RALEIGH (*rising quickly*) Right!

TROTTER. Just wear your belt with revolver case on it. Must have your revolver to shoot rats. And your gas mask—come here —I'll show you. (*He helps Raleigh*) You wear it sort of tucked up under your chin like a serviette.

RALEIGH. Yes. I was shown the way at home.

TROTTER. Now your hat. That's right.

(RALEIGH *picks up his stick*)

You don't want a walking-stick. It gets in your way if you have to run fast.

RALEIGH. Why—er—do you have to run fast?

TROTTER. Oh, Lord, yes, often! If you see a Minnie coming— that's a big trench-mortar shell, you know—short for *Minnywerfer* —you see 'em come right out of the Boche trenches, right up in the air, then down, down, down; and you have to judge it and run like stink sometimes.

(MASON *comes in and down* C *with two cups of coffee*)

MASON (C *to* L) Coffee, sir?

(TROTTER *and* RALEIGH *are* LC. *They both drink and* MASON *waits until they put the mugs back on the tray before he exits*)

TROTTER. Thanks. (*He takes the mug and drinks standing up*)

RALEIGH. Thanks.

TROTTER. You might leave my apricots out, Mason. Put 'em on a separate plate and keep 'em in there. (*He points to Mason's dugout*)

MASON. Very good, sir.

TROTTER. If you bring 'em in 'ere you never know *what* might 'appen to 'em. (*He puts his mug back on the tray*)

(RALEIGH *hands the mug to Mason*)

MASON. No, sir.

(MASON *exit up* L *with the tray*)

TROTTER. 'B' Company on our right, aren't they, skipper?

STANHOPE. Yes. There's fifty yards of undefended area between. You better patrol that a good deal.

TROTTER. Aye, aye, sir.

STANHOPE. Have a look at that Lewis gun position on the left. See what field of fire they've got.

TROTTER. Right sir. By the way. You don't want me to go out and look at that blinkin' ruin?

STANHOPE. I'll see to that.

TROTTER. Good. I don't fancy crawling about on my belly after that cutlet. (*To Raleigh*) Well, come on, my lad, let's go and see about this 'ere war.

(*The two go up the steps,* TROTTER *first, leaving Stanhope and Osborne alone.*
MASON *appears at his dug-out door*)

MASON. Will you take apricots, sir?

STANHOPE. No, thanks.

MASON. Mr Osborne?

OSBORNE. No, thanks.

MASON. I'm sorry about them being apricots, sir. I explained to Mr Osborne——

STANHOPE (*curtly*) That's all right, Mason—thank you.

MASON. Very good, sir.

(MASON *goes out*)

OSBORNE (*over by the bed* R) Will you sleep here? This was Hardy's bed.

STANHOPE. No. You sleep there. I'd rather sleep by the table here. I can get up and work without disturbing you. (*He rises, crosses in front of the table with pack and tries the bed with his hand*)

OSBORNE. This is a better one.

STANHOPE. You take it. Must have a little comfort in your old age, Uncle.

OSBORNE (*crossing back to the bed* L *in front of the table*) I wish you'd turn in and sleep for a bit.

STANHOPE. Sleep?—I can't sleep. (*He takes a whiskey and water*)

(HIBBERT *appears in the trench and comes down the steps—a small, slightly built man in the early twenties, with a little moustache and a pallid face—comes to* RC *by the table, wearing his tin hat and belt, keeping his hat on*)

(*Looking hard at the newcomer*) Well, Hibbert?

HIBBERT. Everything's fairly quiet. Bit of snipping somewhere to our left; some rifle grenades coming over just on our right.

STANHOPE. I see. Mason's got your supper.

HIBBERT (*gently rubbing his forehead*) I don't think I can manage any supper tonight, Stanhope. It's this beastly neuralgia. It seems to be right inside this eye. The beastly pain gets worse every day.

STANHOPE. Some hot soup and a good tough chop'll put that right.

HIBBERT. I'm afraid the pain rather takes my appetite away. I'm damn sorry to keep on talking about it, Stanhope, only I thought you'd wonder why I don't eat anything much.

STANHOPE. Try and forget about it.

HIBBERT (*with a little laugh*) Well—I wish I could.

STANHOPE. Get tight.

HIBBERT (*moving towards dug-out* R) I think I'll turn in for a rest —and try and get some sleep.

STANHOPE. All right. Turn in. You're in that dug-out there. Here's your pack. (*He picks up the pack that Trotter brought down*) You go on duty at two. I take over from you at four. I'll tell Mason to call you.

HIBBERT (*faintly*) Oh, right—thanks, Stanhope—cheero.

(HIBBERT *exits in dug-out* R)

STANHOPE. Cheero. (*He watches* HIBBERT *go down the tunnel into the dark*)

HIBBERT (*returning*) Can I have a candle?

STANHOPE (*kicking box of candles to him from under the table*) Here you are.

HIBBERT. Thanks.

(*After lighting a candle he goes out again. There is silence.* STANHOPE *turns to Osborne*)

STANHOPE. Another little worm trying to wriggle home.

OSBORNE (*filling his pipe*) I wonder if he really is bad. He looks rotten.

STANHOPE. Pure bloody funk, that's all. He could eat if he wanted to; he's starving himself purposely. Artful little swine! Neuralgia's a splendid idea. No proof, as far as I can see.

OSBORNE. You can't help feeling sorry for him. I think he's tried hard.

STANHOPE. How long's he been out here? Three months, I suppose. Now he's decided he's done his bit. He's decided to go home and spend the rest of the war in comfortable nerve hospitals. Well, he's mistaken. I let Warren get away like that, but no more.

OSBORNE. I don't see how you can prevent a fellow going sick.

STANHOPE. I'll have a quiet word with the doctor before *he* does. He thinks he's going to wriggle off before the attack. We'll just see about that. No man of mine's going sick before the attack. They're going to take an equal chance—together. (*He takes out a pocket-book and is writing*)

OSBORNE. Raleigh looks a nice chap.

STANHOPE (*looking hard at Osborne before replying*) Yes.

OSBORNE. Good-looking youngster. At school with you, wasn't he?

STANHOPE (*stops writing and looks at Osborne*) Has he been talking already?

OSBORNE. He just mentioned it. It was a natural thing to tell me when he knew you were in command.

(STANHOPE *is lounging at the table with his back to the wall.* OSBORNE, *sitting on the bed* R, *begins to puff clouds of smoke into the air as he lights his pipe*)

He's awfully pleased to get into your company.

(STANHOPE *makes no reply. He picks up a pencil and scribbles on the back of a magazine*)

He seems to think a lot of you.

STANHOPE (*looking up quickly at Osborne and laughing*) Yes, I'm his hero.

OSBORNE (*leaning back, regarding him*) It's quite natural.

STANHOPE. You think so?

OSBORNE. Small boys at school generally have their heroes.

STANHOPE. Yes. Small boys at school do.

OSBORNE. Often it goes on as long as——

STANHOPE. —as long as the hero's a hero.

OSBORNE. It often goes on all through life.

STANHOPE. I wonder. How many battalions are there in France?

OSBORNE. Why?

STANHOPE. We'll say fifty divisions. That's a hundred and fifty brigades—four hundred and fifty battalions. That's one thousand eight hundred companies. (*He looks up at Osborne from his calculations on the magazine cover*) There are one thousand eight hundred companies in France, Uncle. Raleigh might have been sent to any one of those, and, my God! he comes to mine. (*He drinks—and then slams down the book*)

OSBORNE. You ought to be glad. He's a good-looking youngster. I like him.

STANHOPE. I knew you'd like him. Personality, isn't it? (*He takes a worn leather case from his breast-pocket and hands a small photograph to Osborne*) I've never shown you that, have I?

OSBORNE (*looking at the photograph*) No. (*Pause*)

(STANHOPE *lights a cigarette*)

Raleigh's sister, isn't it?

STANHOPE. How did you know?

OSBORNE. There's a strong likeness.

STANHOPE. I suppose there is.

OSBORNE (*intent on the picture*) She's an awfully nice-looking girl.

STANHOPE. A photo doesn't show much, really. Just a face.

OSBORNE. She looks awfully nice.

(*There is silence.* OSBORNE *hands the photo back*)

You're a lucky chap.

STANHOPE (*putting the photo back into his case*) I don't know why I keep it, really. (*He puts it back in his pocket*)

OSBORNE. Why? Isn't she—I thought——

STANHOPE. What did you think?

OSBORNE. Well, I thought that perhaps she was waiting for you.

STANHOPE. Yes. She is waiting for me—and she doesn't know. She thinks I'm a wonderful chap—commanding a company. (*He turns to Osborne and points up the steps into the line*) She doesn't know that if I went up those steps into the front line—without being doped with whiskey—I'd go mad with fright.

(*There is a pause.* OSBORNE *stirs himself to speak*)

OSBORNE. Look here, old man. I've meant to say it, for a long time, but it sounds damned cheek. You've done longer out here than any man in the battalion. It's time you went away for a rest. It's due to you.

STANHOPE. You suggest that I go sick, like that little worm in there—neuralgia in the eye? (*He laughs and takes a drink*)

OSBORNE. No. Not that. The Colonel would have sent you down long ago, only——

STANHOPE. Only—what?

OSBORNE. Only he can't spare you.

STANHOPE (*laughing*) Oh, rot!

OSBORNE. He told me.

STANHOPE. He thinks I'm in such a state I want a rest, is that it?

OSBORNE. No. He thinks it's due to you.

STANHOPE. It's all right, Uncle. I'll stick it out now. (*He pats his arm*) But it's rather damnable for that boy—of all the boys in the world—to have come to *me*. I might at least have been spared that.

OSBORNE. You're taking rather a dull view of things.

STANHOPE. I've just told you. That boy's a hero-worshipper.

I'm three years older than he is. You know what that means at
school. I was skipper of Rugger and all that sort of thing. It
doesn't sound much to a man out here—but it does at school with
a kid of fourteen. Damn it, Uncle, you're a schoolmaster; you
know.

(OSBORNE *leans back again, watching him*)

OSBORNE. I've just told you what I think of hero-worship.

STANHOPE. Raleigh's father knew mine, and I was told to keep
an eye on the kid. I made him keen on the right things—and all
that. His people asked me to stay with them one summer. I met
his sister then——

OSBORNE. Yes?

STANHOPE. At first I thought of her as another kid like Raleigh.
It was just before I came out here for the first time that I realized
what a topping girl she was. Funny how you realize it suddenly.
I just prayed to come through the war—and—and *do* things—and
keep absolutely fit for her. (*He drinks*)

OSBORNE. You've done pretty well. An M.C. and a company.

STANHOPE (*taking another whiskey*) It was all right at first. When
I went home on leave after six months it was jolly fine to feel I'd
done a little to make her pleased. (*He takes a gulp of his drink*) It
was after I came back here—in that awful affair on Vimy Ridge.
I knew I'd go mad if I didn't break the strain. I couldn't bear
being fully conscious all the time—*you've* felt that, Uncle, haven't
you?

OSBORNE. Yes, often. (*He sits up and thinks*)

STANHOPE. There were only two ways of breaking the strain.
One was pretending I was ill—and going home; the other was
this. (*He holds up his glass*) Which would you pick, Uncle?

OSBORNE. I haven't been through as much as you. I don't
know yet.

STANHOPE. I thought it all out. It's a slimy thing to go home if
you're not really ill, isn't it?

OSBORNE. I think it is.

STANHOPE. Well, then. (*He holds his glass up to Osborne*) Cheero,
and long live the men who go home with neuralgia. (*He puts his
glass down*) I didn't go home on my last leave. I couldn't bear to
meet her, in case she realized——

OSBORNE. When the war's over—and the strain's gone—you'll
soon be as fit as ever, at your age. (*He leans back*)

STANHOPE. I've hoped that all the time. I'd go away for months
and live in the open air—and get fit—and then go back to her.

OSBORNE. And so you can.

STANHOPE. If Raleigh had gone to one of those other one thousand eight hundred companies.

OSBORNE. I don't see why you should think——

STANHOPE. Oh, for Lord's sake don't be a damn fool. (*He leans forward*) *You* know! You know he'll write and tell her I reek of whiskey all day.

OSBORNE. Why should he? He's not a——

STANHOPE. Exactly. He's not a damned little swine who'd deceive his sister.

OSBORNE. He's very young; he's got hundreds of strange things to learn; he'll realize that men are—*different*—out here.

STANHOPE. It's no good, Uncle. Didn't you see him sitting there at supper?—staring at me?—and wondering? He's up in those trenches now—still wondering—and beginning to understand. And all these months he's wanted to be with me out here. Poor little devil! (*He drinks*)

OSBORNE. I believe Raleigh'll go on liking you—and looking up to you—through everything. There's something very deep, and rather fine, about hero-worship.

STANHOPE. Hero-worship be damned! (*He pauses, then goes on, in a strange, high-pitched voice*) You know, Uncle, I'm an *awful* fool. I'm *captain* of this company. What the hell's that bloody little prig of a boy matter? D'you see? He's a little prig. Wants to write home and tell Madge all about *me*. Well, he won't; d'you see, Uncle? He *won't* write. Censorship! I censor his letters—cross out all he says about me.

OSBORNE. You can't read his letters.

STANHOPE (*dreamily*) Cross out all he says about me. Then we all go west in the big attack—and she goes on thinking I'm a fine fellow for ever—and ever—and ever. (*He pours out a drink, murmuring* 'Ever—and ever—and ever')

OSBORNE (*rising*) It's not as bad as all that. Turn in and have a sleep. (*He puts the coat on the bed for a pillow, then puts his hand on Stanhope*)

STANHOPE. Sleep! Catch *me* wasting my time with sleep.

OSBORNE (*picking up Stanhope's pack and pulling out the blanket*) Come along, old chap. You come and lie down here. (*He puts the pack as a pillow on Stanhope's bed, and spreads out the blanket*)

STANHOPE (*with his chin in his hands*) Little prig—that's what he is. Did *I* ask him to force his way into my company? No! I didn't. Very well, he'll pay for his damn cheek.

(OSBORNE *lays his hand gently on Stanhope's shoulder to persuade him to lie down*)

Go away! (*He shakes Osborne's hand off*) What the hell are you trying to do?

OSBORNE. Come and lie down and go to sleep.

STANHOPE. Go sleep y'self. I censor his letters, d'you see, Uncle? You watch and see he doesn't smuggle any letters away.

OSBORNE. Righto. Now come and lie down. You've had a hard day of it.

(*Machine-gun fires*)

STANHOPE (*looking up suddenly*) Where's Hardy? (*He rises*) D'you say he's gone?

OSBORNE. Yes. He's gone.

STANHOPE. Gone, has he? (*He turns to the entrance*) Y'know, I had a word to say to Master Hardy. He would go, the swine! Dirty trenches—everything dirty—I wanner tell him to keep his trenches clean.

OSBORNE (*going to him and stopping him, standing beside Stanhope and putting his hand gently on his shoulder again*) We'll clean them up tomorrow.

(STANHOPE *looks up at Osborne and laughs gaily*)

STANHOPE. Dear old Uncle! Clean trenches up—with a little dustpan and brush. (*He laughs*) Make you little apron—with lace on it.

OSBORNE. That'll be fine. (*He leads Stanhope to the bed* L) Now then, come along, old chap. I'll see you get called at two o'clock. (*He firmly takes Stanhope by the arm and draws him over to the bed*) You *must* be tired.

STANHOPE (*in a dull voice*) God, I'm bloody tired; ache—all over —feel sick.

(OSBORNE *helps him to the bed, lifts his legs and lays him on the bed, gets his warm from up* C, *takes the blanket and puts it over him*)

OSBORNE. You'll feel all right in a minute. How's that? Comfortable?

STANHOPE. Yes. Comfortable. (*He looks up into Osborne's face and laughs again*) Dear old Uncle. Tuck me up.

(OSBORNE *fumbles the blankets round Stanhope*)

OSBORNE. There we are.

STANHOPE. Kiss me, Uncle.

OSBORNE. Kiss you be blowed! You go to sleep.

STANHOPE (*closing his eyes*) Yes—I go sleep. (*He turns slowly on to his* R *side with his face to the earth wall*)

(OSBORNE *stands watching for a while, then blows out the candle by Stanhope's bed.* STANHOPE *gives a deep sigh, and begins to breathe heavily.* OSBORNE *goes to the servant's dug-out and calls softly*)

OSBORNE. Mason!

MASON (*appearing with unbuttoned tunic up* L *at the tunnel entrance*) Yessir?

OSBORNE. Will you call me at ten minutes to eleven—and Mr Hibbert at ten minutes to two? I'm going to turn in for a little while.

MASON. Very good, sir. (*Pause*) The pepper's come, sir.

OSBORNE. Oh, good.

MASON. I'm very sorry about the pepper, sir.

OSBORNE. That's all right, Mason.
MASON. Good night, sir.
OSBORNE. Good night.

(*Guns are heard off, softly.*

MASON *exits.* OSBORNE *turns, and looks up the narrow steps into the night, where the 'Verey' lights rise and fade against the starlit sky. He glances once more at Stanhope, then crosses to his own bed, takes out from his tunic pocket a large, old-fashioned watch, and quietly winds it up.*

Through the stillness comes the low rumble of distant guns)

The CURTAIN *falls*

ACT II

SCENE I

SCENE—*Early next morning.*

There is no machine gun heard in this scene, merely the drum to give effect of gunfire, carried by the wind.

A pale shaft of sunlight shines down the steps, but candles still burn in the dark corner where OSBORNE *and* RALEIGH *are discovered at breakfast.* RALEIGH *is sitting on* L *of table.* OSBORNE C *at back of table.* MASON *has put a large plate of bacon before each, and turns to go as* TROTTER *enters, comes down the steps, whistling gaily and rubbing his hands.*

TROTTER (*taking off his belt and putting it on the bed*) What a lovely smell of bacon!

MASON. Yes, sir. I reckon there's enough smell of bacon in 'ere to last for dinner.

TROTTER. Well, there's nothing like a good fat bacon rasher when you're as empty as I am.

MASON. I'm glad you like it fat, sir.

TROTTER. Well, I like a bit o' lean, too.

MASON. There *was* a bit of lean in the middle of yours, sir, but it's kind of shrunk up in the cooking.

TROTTER (*sitting* R *of the table*) Bad cooking, that's all. Any porridge?

MASON. Oh, yes, sir. There's porridge.

TROTTER. Lumpy, I s'pose?

MASON. Yes, sir. Quite nice and lumpy. (*He stands behind to attention*)

TROTTER. Well, take the lumps out o' mine.

MASON. And just bring you the gravy, sir? Very good, sir.

(MASON *goes out.* TROTTER *looks after him suspiciously*)

TROTTER. You know, that man's getting familiar.

OSBORNE. He's not a bad cook.

(TROTTER *has picked up his coffee-mug, and is smelling it*)

TROTTER. I say, d'you realize he's washed his dish-cloth?

OSBORNE. I know. I told him about it.

TROTTER. Did you really? You've got some pluck. 'Ow did you go about it? (*He drinks*)

OSBORNE. I wrote and asked my wife for a packet of Lux. Then I gave it to Mason and suggested he tried it on something.

TROTTER. Good man. No, he's not a bad cook as cooks go. Might be a lot worse. When I was in the ranks we 'ad a prize cook

27

—used to be a plumber before the war. Ought to 'ave seen the stew 'e made. Thin! Thin wasn't the word. Put a bucketful of 'is stew in a bath and ·pull the plug, and the whole lot would go down in a couple of gurgles.

(MASON *brings Trotter's porridge*)

MASON. I've took the lumps out. (*He stands behind Trotter*)
TROTTER. Good. Keep 'em and use 'em for dumplings next time we 'ave boiled beef.
MASON. Very good, sir.

(MASON *goes out*)

TROTTER. Yes. That plumber was a prize cook, 'e was. Lucky for us, one day 'e set 'imself on fire making the tea. 'E went 'ome properly fried. Did Mason get that pepper?
OSBORNE. Yes.
TROTTER (*quickly*) Good. Must 'ave pepper.
OSBORNE. I thought you were on duty now.
TROTTER. I'm supposed to be. Stanhope sent me down to get my breakfast. He's looking after things till I finish.
OSBORNE. He's got a long job then.
TROTTER. Oh, no. I'm a quick eater. Hi! Mason! Bacon!
MASON (*outside*) Coming, sir!
OSBORNE. It's a wonderful morning.
TROTTER. Isn't it lovely? Makes you feel sort of young and 'opeful. I was up in that old trench under the brick wall just now, and damned if a bloomin' little bird didn't start singing!

(MASON *enters with Trotter's bacon*)

Didn't 'arf sound funny. Sign of spring, I s'pose. (*He looks at the plate*) That looks all right.
MASON (*leaning over*) If you look down straight on it from above, sir, you can see the bit o' lean quite clear.
TROTTER. Good Lord, yes! That's it, isn't it?
MASON. No, sir; that's a bit o' rust off the pan.
TROTTER. Ah! *That's* it, then!
MASON. You've got it, sir.

(MASON *exits*)

TROTTER. Cut us a chunk of bread, Uncle.

(OSBORNE *throws him a biscuit, which must fall with a clatter on the plate*)

OSBORNE. How are things going up there?
TROTTER. I don't like the look of things a bit.
OSBORNE. You mean—the quiet?
TROTTER. Yes. Standing up there in the dark last night there didn't seem a thing in the world alive—except the rats squeaking and my stomach grumbling about that cutlet.

OSBORNE. It's quiet even now.

TROTTER. Too damn quiet.

(*Electrics Cue No.* 1)

You can bet your boots the Boche is up to something. The big attack soon, I reckon. I don't like it, Uncle. Pass the jam.

OSBORNE. It's strawberry.

TROTTER. Is it? I'm glad we've got rid o' that raspberry jam. Can't stand raspberry jam. Pips get be'ind your plate.

OSBORNE. Did Stanhope tell you he wants two wiring parties out tonight?

TROTTER. Yes. He's fixing it up now. (*He pauses, and goes on in a low voice*) My goodness, Uncle, doesn't he look ill!

OSBORNE. I'm afraid he's not well.

TROTTER. Nobody'd be well who went on like he does. (*There is another pause*) You know when you came up to relieve me last night?

OSBORNE. Yes?

TROTTER. Well, Raleigh and me came back here, and there was Stanhope sitting on that bed drinking a whiskey. He looked as white as a sheet. God, he looked awful; he'd drunk the bottle since dinner. I said, "'Ullo!' and he didn't seem to know who I was. Uncanny, wasn't it, Raleigh?

RALEIGH (*with lowered head*) Yes.

TROTTER. He just said, 'Better go to bed, Raleigh'—just as if Raleigh'd been a school kid.

(*Cue* 1 *must finish here*)

OSBORNE. Did he? (*There is a pause*) Look at the sun. It'll be quite warm soon.

(*They look at the pale square of sunlight on the floor*)

TROTTER. It's warm now. You can feel it on your face outside if you stand in it. First time this year. 'Ope we 'ave an 'ot summer (*He rubs his hands and sprawls out his feet*)

OSBORNE. So do I.

TROTTER. Funny about that bird. Made me feel quite braced up. Sort of made me think about my garden of an evening— walking round in me slippers after supper, smoking me pipe.

OSBORNE. You keen on gardening?

TROTTER. Oh, I used to do a bit of an evening. I 'ad a decent little grass plot in front, with flower-borders—geraniums, lobelia, and calceolaria—you know, red, white, and blue. Lovely.

OSBORNE. Yes.

TROTTER. 'Ad some fine 'olly'ocks out the back. One year I 'ad one eight feet 'igh. Took a photer of it. (*He fumbles in his pocket-case*) Like to look at it?

OSBORNE. I would. (*He looks at the photo*) By Jove, it's a beauty.

TROTTER (*attracting Raleigh's attention*) 'Ere, Raleigh, 'olly'ock. (*He looks over Osborne's shoulder*) You see that, just there?

OSBORNE. Yes?

TROTTER. That's the roof of the summer-'ouse.

OSBORNE. Is it really!

TROTTER. Just shows the 'ite of the 'olly'ock. (*He coughs out some biscuit*)

OSBORNE. It does. (*He shows the photo to Raleigh*) A beauty, isn't it?

RALEIGH. Rather!

TROTTER. It never wanted no stick to keep it straight, neether. (*There is a pause*) You keen on gardening?

OSBORNE. Yes. A bit. I made a rockery when I was home on leave. I used to cycle out to the woods and get primroses and things like that, and try and get 'em to grow in my garden.

TROTTER. I don't suppose they would!

OSBORNE. They would if you pressed a bit of moss round them——

TROTTER. —to make 'em feel at 'ome, eh? (*He drinks and laughs*)

OSBORNE. They'll be coming out again soon if they've got this sun at home.

TROTTER. I reckon they will. I remember one morning last spring—we was coming out of the salient. Just when it was getting light in the morning—it was the time when the Boche was sending over a lot of that gas that smells like pear-drops, you know?

OSBORNE. I know. Phosgene.

TROTTER. That's it. We were scared to hell of it. All of a sudden we smelt that funny sweet smell, and a fellow shouted 'Gas!'— and we put on our masks; and then I spotted what it was.

OSBORNE. What was it?

TROTTER. Why, a blinkin' may-tree! All out in bloom, growing beside the path! We did feel a lot of silly poops—putting on gas masks because of a damn may-tree! (*He stretches himself and tries to button his tunic*) Lord! I *must* get my fat down. (*He rises, stretches himself, goes over to bed R and puts kit on*) Well, I better go and relieve Stanhope. He'll curse like hell if I don't. I bet he's got a red-hot liver this morning.

OSBORNE. I relieve you at eleven.

TROTTER. That's right. (*He moves over RC, faces the other two as he dresses*) I don't like this time of day in the line. The old Boche 'as just 'ad 'is breakfast, and sends over a few whizz-bangs and rifle grenades to show 'e ain't forgotten us. Still, I'd rather 'ave a bang or two than this damn quiet. (*He puts on his helmet and gas mask satchel and goes up the steps*) Cheero!

OSBORNE. Cheero!

RALEIGH. Cheero!

OSBORNE (*to Raleigh*) I expect Stanhope'll let you go on duty alone now.

Raleigh. Will he? About what time?

Osborne. Well, after me, I expect. From about two till four.

Raleigh. I see.

(*There is a pause. Then* Osborne *looks at Raleigh and laughs*)

Osborne. What do you think about it all?

Raleigh. Oh, all right, thanks. (*He laughs as he fills his pipe*) I feel I've been here ages.

Osborne (*filling his pipe*) I expect you do. The time passes, though.

Raleigh. Are we here for six days?

Osborne. Yes. Seems a long time, doesn't it?

Raleigh (*laughing shortly*) It does rather. I can't imagine—the end of six days here——

Osborne. Anyhow, we've done twelve hours already. It's fine when you are relieved and go down the line to billets, and have a good hot bath, and sit and read under trees.

Raleigh (*the thought strikes him suddenly*) Good Lord, I feel I haven't seen a tree for ages—not a real tree, with leaves and branches—and yet I've only been here twelve hours.

Osborne. How did you feel—in the front line?

Raleigh. Oh, all right. It seemed so frightfully quiet and uncanny—everybody creeping about and talking in low voices. I suppose you've *got* to talk quietly when you're so near the German front line—only about seventy yards, isn't it?

Osborne. Yes. About the breadth of a Rugger field.

Raleigh. It's funny to think of it like that.

Osborne. I always measure distances like that out here. Keeps them in proportion.

Raleigh. Did you play Rugger?

Osborne. Yes. But mostly reffing at school in the last few years.

Raleigh. Are you a schoolmaster, then?

Osborne. Yes. I must apologize.

Raleigh. Oh, I don't mind schoolmasters. (*He puts his hands to his mouth, realizing his mistake. Hastily*) I—I—mean, I never met one outside a school.

Osborne. They do get out sometimes.

Raleigh (*laughing*) Who did you play for?

Osborne. The Harlequins.

Raleigh. Did you?

Osborne. I played for the English team on one great occasion.

Raleigh. What! For *England*!

Osborne. I was awfully lucky to get the chance. It's a long time ago now.

Raleigh (*with awe*) Oh, but, good Lord! that must have been simply topping. Where did you play?

Osborne. Wing three.

Raleigh. I say, I—I never realized—you'd played for England.

Osborne. Tuppence to talk to me now! Anyhow, don't breeze it about.

Raleigh. Don't the others know?

Osborne. We never talk about Rugger.

Raleigh. They ought to know. It'd make them feel jolly bucked.

Osborne (*laughing*) It doesn't make much difference out here!

Raleigh. It must be awfully thrilling, playing in front of a huge crowd—all shouting and cheering——

Osborne. You don't notice it when the game begins.

Raleigh. You're too taken up with the game?

Osborne. Yes.

Raleigh. I used to get wind up playing at school with only a few kids looking on.

Osborne. You feel it more when there are only a few. (*He has picked up a slip of paper from the table; suddenly he laughs*) Look at this!

Raleigh (*looking at it curiously*) What is it?

Osborne. Trotter's plan to make the time pass quickly. One hundred and forty-four little circles—one for each hour of six days. He's blacked in six already. He's six hours behind.

Raleigh. It's rather a good idea. I like Trotter.

Osborne. He's a good chap.

Raleigh. He makes things feel—natural.

Osborne. He's a genuine sort of chap.

Raleigh. That's it. He's genuine. (*There is a long pause. He has been filling a new pipe*)

(Osborne *is puffing at his old one*)

How topping—to have played for England!

Osborne. It *was* rather fun.

(*Two bangs go with a whistle*)

Raleigh (*after a pause*) The Germans are really quite decent, aren't they? I mean, outside the newspapers?

Osborne. Yes. (*Pause*) I remember up at Wipers we had a man shot when he was out on patrol. Just at dawn. We couldn't get him in that night. He lay out there groaning all day. Next night three of our men crawled out to get him in. It was so near the German trenches that they could have shot our fellows one by one. But, when our men began dragging the wounded man back over the rough ground, a big German officer stood up in their trenches and called out: 'Carry him!'—and our fellows stood up and carried the man back, and the German officer fired some lights for them to see by.

Raleigh. Really!

Osborne. Next day we blew each other's trenches to blazes.

Raleigh. It all seems rather—*silly*, doesn't it?

Osborne. It does, rather.

(*There is silence for a while*)

RALEIGH. I started a letter when I came off duty last night. How do we send letters?

OSBORNE. The Quartermaster-Sergeant takes them down after he brings rations up in the evenings.

(STANHOPE *enters from the trench above and comes slowly down the steps.* RALEIGH *rises*)

RALEIGH. I think I'll go and finish it now—if I go on duty soon.

OSBORNE. Come and write it in here. It's more cheery.

RALEIGH. It's all right, thanks; I'm quite comfortable in there. I've rigged up a sort of little table beside my bed.

OSBORNE. Righto.

(RALEIGH *goes into his dug-out.* STANHOPE *is slowly taking off his equipment*)

STANHOPE. What a foul smell of bacon.

OSBORNE. Yes. We've got bacon for breakfast.

STANHOPE. So I gather. Have you told Raleigh about rifle inspection?

OSBORNE. No.

STANHOPE (*at the entrance to Raleigh's dug-out*) Raleigh!

RALEIGH (*appearing in doorway to the dug-out*) Yes?

STANHOPE. You inspect your platoon's rifles at nine o'clock.

RALEIGH. Oh, righto, Stanhope. (*He goes back again*)

STANHOPE (*sitting at the table*) I've arranged two wiring parties to begin at eight o'clock tonight—Corporal Burt with two men and Sergeant Smith with two. I want them to strengthen the wire all along the front.

OSBORNE. It's very weak at present.

STANHOPE. Every company leaves it for the next one to do. There's great holes blown out weeks ago.

OSBORNE. I know.

STANHOPE. Next night we'll start putting a belt of wire down both flanks.

OSBORNE. Down the flanks!

STANHOPE. Yes. We'll wire ourselves right in. If this attack comes I'm not going to trust the companies on our sides to hold their ground.

(MASON *has come in, and stands diffidently in the background*)

MASON. Would you like a nice bit o' bacon, sir?

STANHOPE. No, thanks. I'll have a cup of tea.

MASON. Right, sir.

(MASON *goes out*)

STANHOPE. I've been having a good look round. We've got a

strong position here—if we wire ourselves right in. The Colonel's
been talking to me up there.

OSBORNE. Oh. Has he been round?

STANHOPE. Yes. He says a German prisoner gave the day of
attack as the twenty-first.

Osborne. That's Thursday?

STANHOPE. Yes. Today's Tuesday.

OSBORNE. That means about dawn the day after tomorrow.

STANHOPE. The second dawn from now.

(*There is a pause*)

OSBORNE. Then it'll come while we're here.

STANHOPE. Yes. It'll come while we're here. And we shall be
in the front row of the stalls.

OSBORNE. Oh, well——

(*In the silence that follows,* MASON *enters with a cup of tea to
behind the table*)

MASON. Would you like a nice plate of sardines, sir?

STANHOPE. I should loathe it.

MASON. Very good, sir.

(MASON *goes out*)

OSBORNE. Did the Colonel have much to say?

STANHOPE. Only that when the attack comes we can't expect
any help from behind. We're not to move from here. We've got
to stick it.

OSBORNE. I see.

STANHOPE. We'll wire ourselves in as strongly as possible. I've
got to arrange battle positions for each platoon and section this
afternoon.

OSBORNE. Well, I'm glad it's coming at last. I'm sick of waiting.

STANHOPE (*looking at Trotter's chart*) Good Lord! What on
earth's this extraordinary affair?

OSBORNE. Trotter's plan to make the time pass by. A hundred
and forty-four circles—one for each hour of six days.

STANHOPE. How many hours are there till dawn on the twenty-
first?

OSBORNE. Goodness knows. Not many, I hope.

STANHOPE. Nearly nine o'clock now. Twenty-four till nine tomorrow; twelve till nine at night—that's thirty-six; nine till six
next morning; that's forty-five altogether. (*He begins to count off
forty-five circles on Trotter's chart*)

OSBORNE. What are you going to do?

STANHOPE. At the end of the forty-fifth circle I'm going to draw
a picture of Trotter being blown up in four pieces.

OSBORNE. Don't spoil his chart. It took him an hour to make
that.

Stanhope. He won't see the point. He's no imagination.

Osborne. I don't suppose he has.

Stanhope. Funny not to have any imagination. Must be rather nice.

Osborne. A bit dull, I should think.

Stanhope. It must be, rather. I suppose all his life Trotter feels like you and I do when we're drowsily drunk.

Osborne. Poor chap!

Stanhope. I suppose if Trotter looks at that wall he just sees a brown surface. He doesn't see into the earth beyond—the worms wandering about round the stones and roots of trees. I wonder how a worm knows when it's going up or down.

Osborne. When it's going down I suppose the blood runs into its head and makes it throb.

Stanhope. Worms haven't got any blood.

Osborne. Then I don't suppose it ever does know.

Stanhope. Rotten if it didn't—and went on going down when it thought it was coming up.

Osborne. Yes. I expect that's the one thing worms dread.

Stanhope. D'you think this life sharpens the imagination?

Osborne. It must.

Stanhope. Whenever I look at anything nowadays I see right through it. Looking at you now, there's your uniform—your jersey—shirt—vest—then beyond that——

Osborne. Let's talk about something else——

Stanhope (*laughing*) Sorry! It's a habit that's grown on me lately—to look right through things, and on and on—till I get frightened and stop.

Osborne. I suppose everybody out here—*feels* more keenly.

Stanhope. I hope so. I wondered if there was anything wrong with me. D'you ever get a sudden feeling that everything's going farther and farther away—till you're the only thing in the world —and then the world begins going away—until you're the only thing in—in the universe—and you struggle to get back—and can't?

Osborne. Bit of nerve strain, that's all.

Stanhope. You don't think I'm going potty?

Osborne. Oh, Lord, no!

Stanhope (*throwing back his head and laughing*) Dear old Uncle! you don't really know, do you? You just pretend you do, to make me feel all right.

Osborne. When people are going potty they never talk about it; they keep it to themselves.

Stanhope. Oh, well, that's all right, then. (*There is silence for a while*) I had that feeling this morning, standing out there in the line while the sun was rising. By the way, did you see the sunrise? Wasn't it gorgeous?

Osborne. Splendid—this morning.

STANHOPE. I was looking across at the Boche trenches and right beyond—not a sound or a soul; just an enormous plain, all churned up like a sea that's got muddier and muddier till it's so stiff that it can't move. You could have heard a pin drop in the quiet; yet you knew thousands of guns were hidden there, all ready cleaned and oiled—millions of bullets lying in pouches—thousands of Germans, waiting and thinking. Then, gradually, that feeling came——

OSBORNE. I never knew the sun could rise in so many ways till I came out here. Green, and pink, and red, and blue, and grey. Extraordinary, isn't it?

STANHOPE. Yes. Hi! Mason!

MASON (answering from outside) Yessir!

STANHOPE. Bring some mugs and a bottle of whiskey.

MASON. Yessir.

OSBORNE (smiling) So early in the morning?

STANHOPE. Just a spot. It's damn cold in here.

OSBORNE (turning over the pages of a magazine) This show at the Hippodrome has been running a long time.

STANHOPE. What? Zig-zag?

OSBORNE. Yes. George Robey's in it.

STANHOPE. Harper saw it on leave. Says it's damn good. Robey's pricelessly funny.

(MASON brings whiskey and mugs, then exits)

OSBORNE. Wish I'd seen a show on leave.

STANHOPE. D'you mean to say you didn't go to any shows?

OSBORNE (laughing) No. I spent all the time in the garden, making a rockery. In the evenings I used to sit and smoke and read—and my wife used to knit socks and play the piano a bit. We pretended there wasn't any war at all—till my two youngsters made me help in a tin-soldier battle on the floor.

STANHOPE. Poor old Uncle! You can't get away from it, can you?

OSBORNE. I wish I knew how to fight a battle like those boys of mine. You ought to have seen the way they lured my men under the sofa and mowed them down.

STANHOPE (laughing and helping himself to a drink) You going to have one?

OSBORNE. Not now, thanks.

STANHOPE. You go on duty at eleven, don't you?

OSBORNE. Yes. I relieve Trotter.

STANHOPE. Raleigh better go on at one o'clock and stay with you for an hour. Then he can stay on alone till four. Hibbert relieves him at four.

OSBORNE. Righto.

STANHOPE. What's Raleigh doing now?

OSBORNE. Finishing a letter.

STANHOPE. Did you tell him?

OSBORNE. About what?

STANHOPE. Censorship.

OSBORNE. You don't mean that seriously?

STANHOPE. Mean it? Of course I meant it.

OSBORNE. You can't read his letters.

STANHOPE. Officially I'm supposed to read all your letters. Damn it all, Uncle! Imagine yourself in my place—a letter going away from here—from that boy——

OSBORNE. He'll say nothing—rotten—about you.

STANHOPE. You think so? (*There is a pause*) I heard you go on duty last night. After you'd gone, I got up. I was feeling bad. I forgot Raleigh was out there with Trotter. I'd forgotten all about him. I was sleepy. I just knew something beastly had happened. Then he came in with Trotter—and looked at me. After coming in out of the night air, this place must have reeked of candle grease, and rats—and whiskey. He looked at me as if I'd hit him between the eyes—as if I'd spat on him——

OSBORNE. You imagine things.

STANHOPE (*laughing*) Imagine things! No need to imagine!

OSBORNE. Why can't you treat him like any other youngster?

(RALEIGH *comes in from his dug-out with a letter in his hand. He stops short as he notices the abrupt silence that follows his entry*)

RALEIGH. I'm sorry.

OSBORNE. It's all right, Raleigh. Going to inspect rifles?

RALEIGH. Yes.

OSBORNE. You needn't bother if the wood's a bit dirty—just the barrels and magazines and all the metal parts.

RALEIGH. Righto.

OSBORNE. See there's plenty of oil on it. And look at the ammunition in the men's pouches.

RALEIGH. Right. (*He turns up to go out, stops, feels in his pocket, then turns and faces the others again*) Where do we put the letters to be collected?

OSBORNE. Oh, just on the table.

RALEIGH. Thanks. (*He begins to lick the flap of the envelope*)

STANHOPE (*in a quiet voice*) You leave it open.

RALEIGH (*surprised*) Open? (*He stops* RC, *faces the other two*)

STANHOPE. Yes. I have to censor all letters.

RALEIGH (*stammering*) Oh, but—I haven't said anything about —where we are——

STANHOPE. It's the rule that letters must be read.

RALEIGH (*nervously*) Oh, I—I didn't realize that. (*He stands embarrassed; then gives a short laugh*) I—I think—I'll just leave it, then. (*He unbuttons his tunic pocket to put the letter away*)

(*As* RALEIGH *unbuttons his tunic to put the letter back* STANHOPE *jumps up and over to him. They are both* RC)

STANHOPE. Give me that letter!

RALEIGH (*astonished*) But—Dennis——

STANHOPE (*trembling*) Give me that letter!

RALEIGH. But it's—it's private. I didn't know——

STANHOPE. D'you understand an order? Give me that letter!

RALEIGH. But I tell you—there's nothing—— (*He backs away*)

(STANHOPE *rushes at him, clutches Raleigh's wrist and tears the letter from his hand*)

Dennis—I'm——

STANHOPE. Don't 'Dennis' me! Stanhope's my name! You're not at school! Go and inspect your rifles!

(RALEIGH *stands in amazement at the foot of the steps*)

(*Shouting*) D'you understand an order?

(*For a moment* RALEIGH *stares wide-eyed at* STANHOPE, *who is trembling and breathing heavily, then almost in a whisper he says:* 'Right,' *and goes quietly up the narrow steps.* STANHOPE *turns towards the table*)

OSBORNE. Good heavens, Stanhope!

STANHOPE (*wheeling furiously on Osborne*) Look here, Osborne, I'm commanding this company. I ask for advice when I want it!

OSBORNE. Very well.

(STANHOPE *sinks down at the* L *of the table with the letter in his hand. There is silence for a moment. Then he throws the letter on the table and rests his head between his hands*)

STANHOPE. Oh, God! I don't want to read the blasted thing!

OSBORNE. You'll let it go, then?

STANHOPE. I don't care. (*There is a pause*)

OSBORNE. Shall I glance through it—for you?

STANHOPE. If you like.

OSBORNE. I don't *want* to.

STANHOPE. You better. I can't. (*He rises and moves restlessly about, then sits on bed* L *of the table*)

(OSBORNE *takes the letter from the table and opens it.* STANHOPE *sits with his head in his hand, digging a magazine with a pencil. After a while* OSBORNE *glances up at Stanhope*)

OSBORNE. D'you want to hear?

STANHOPE. I suppose I better know.

OSBORNE. He begins with a description of his getting here—he doesn't mention the names of any places.

STANHOPE. What does he say then?

OSBORNE. The last piece is about you.

STANHOPE. Go on.

OSBORNE (*reading*) He says: 'And now I come to the great news.

I reported at Battalion Headquarters, and the Colonel looked in a little book, and said, "You report to 'C' Company—Captain Stanhope." Can't you imagine what I felt? I was taken along some trenches and shown a dug-out. There was an awfully nice officer there—quite old—with grey hair'—(*He clears his throat*)—'and then later Dennis came in. He looked tired, but that's because he works so frightfully hard, and because of the responsibility. Then I went on duty in the front line, and a sergeant told me all about Dennis. He said that Dennis is the finest officer in the battalion, and the men simply love him. He hardly ever sleeps in the dug-out; he's always up in the front line with the men, cheering them on with jokes, and making them keen about things, like he did the kids at school. I'm awfully proud to think he's my friend.'

(*There is silence. Stanhope has not moved while Osborne has read*)

That's all. (*Pause. He puts it down quietly*) Shall I stick it down?

(STANHOPE *sits with lowered head. He murmurs something that sounds like* 'Yes, please.' *He rises heavily and crosses to the shadows by Osborne's bed.*
The sun is shining quite brightly in the trench outside)

The CURTAIN *falls*

SCENE 2

SCENE—*Afternoon on the same day. The sunlight has gone from the dug-out floor, but still shines brightly in the trench.*
The box used above the table is brought to below the table (C *of*) *and another box* (*bigger*) *is brought on from off* L *and placed behind table* (C *of*). *The bed* L *is pushed back slightly.*
STANHOPE *is lying on his bed* L *reading by the light of a candle on the table beside him. A burly* FIGURE *comes groping down the steps and stands blinking in the shadows of the dug-out. The* SERGEANT-MAJOR *is a huge man, with a heavy black moustache, a fat red face, and massive chin.*
STANHOPE *puts the magazine down, rises, and sits up to the table* L *of same.*

STANHOPE. I want to talk with you, Sergeant-Major.
SERGEANT-MAJOR (*standing stolidly by the steps*) Yes, sir?
STANHOPE. Sit down. Have a whiskey?
SERGEANT-MAJOR (*a suspicion of brightness in his voice*) Thank you, sir.

(*The* SERGEANT-MAJOR *sits on the box* R *of table and diffidently takes a small tot*)

STANHOPE. I say. You won't taste that. Take a proper one.
SERGEANT-MAJOR. Well—sir——

(STANHOPE *reaches over, helps the Sergeant-Major to a large tot,
who then takes a big pull.* STANHOPE *watches him, smiles, and takes
one himself*

Turning chilly again, sir. Quite warm this morning.
STANHOPE. Yes.
SERGEANT-MAJOR. Well, here's your very good health, sir. (*He
raises his glass and drinks*)
STANHOPE. Cheero. (*He puts down his glass and abruptly changes his
tone*) Now, look here (*placing map on the box* C *of table and refers to
it*), Sergeant-Major. We must expect this attack on Thursday
morning, at dawn. That's the second dawn from now.

(*The* SERGEANT-MAJOR *brings his box forward and sits facing
Stanhope, then reaches over and puts a candle from the table on the box;
takes a very dirty little note-book from his pocket and jots down notes
with a very small stub of pencil*)

SERGEANT-MAJOR. Thursday morning. Very good, sir.
STANHOPE. We're to hold these trenches, and no man's to move
from here.
SERGEANT-MAJOR. Right, sir.
STANHOPE. It may happen that companies on our sides will
give way, leaving our flanks exposed; so I want a screen of wire
put down both flanks till it meets the wire in the support line.
SERGEANT-MAJOR (*writing hurriedly*) Both flanks—yes, sir.
STANHOPE. When the attack begins, I shall take charge of the
left, and Mr Osborne the right. You will be with Mr Osborne,
and Sergeant Baker with me; Nine and Ten Platoons will move
over here (*pointing out the position on the trench map*); Eleven and
Twelve Platoons to the left.
SERGEANT-MAJOR. Nine, Ten, Eleven and Twelve. I see, sir!
(*He leans back*)
STANHOPE. Is there anything you're not clear about?
SERGEANT-MAJOR (*looking at his notes*) Seems all clear, sir.
STANHOPE. Anything you want to know?
SERGEANT-MAJOR. Well, sir (*clearing his throat*)—when the
attack comes, of course, we beat 'em off (*leaning forward*)—but
what if they keep on attacking?
STANHOPE. Then we keep on beating them off.
SERGEANT-MAJOR. Yes, sir. But what I mean is—they're bound
to make a big thing of it.
STANHOPE (*cheerily*) Oh, I think they will!
SERGEANT-MAJOR. Well, then, sir. If they don't get through the
first day, they'll attack the next day and the next——
STANHOPE. They're bound to.

SERGEANT-MAJOR. Then oughtn't we to fix up something about, well (*he gropes for the right words*)—er—falling back?

STANHOPE. There's no need to—you see, this company's stronger than 'A' and 'B' Companies on either side of us.

SERGEANT-MAJOR. Quite, sir.

STANHOPE. Well, then, if anyone breaks, 'A' and 'B' will break before we do. As long as we stick here when the other companies have given way, we can fire into the Boche as they try and get through the gaps on our sides—we'll make a hell of a mess of them. We might delay the advance a whole day.

SERGEANT-MAJOR (*diffidently*) Yes, sir, but what 'appens when the Boche 'as all got round the back of us?

STANHOPE. Then we advance and win the war.

SERGEANT-MAJOR. Win the war. Very good, sir. (*He makes a note in the book quickly*)

STANHOPE. But you understand exactly what I mean, Sergeant-Major. Our orders are to stick here. If you're told to stick where you.are you don't make plans to retire.

SERGEANT-MAJOR. No, sir.

(OSBORNE's *voice is heard calling down the steps.* SERGEANT-MAJOR *rises, and puts the box back to* R *of the table*)

OSBORNE. Are you there, Stanhope?

STANHOPE (*rising quickly*) Yes. What's the matter?

OSBORNE. The Colonel's up here. Wants to see you——

STANHOPE. Oh, right, I'll come up.

(SERGEANT-MAJOR *rises and replaces the box. He stands* LC)

COLONEL (*from above*) All right, Stanhope—I'll come down.

SERGEANT-MAJOR (*who has risen*) Anything more, sir?

STANHOPE. I don't think so. I'll see you at stand-to this evening.

SERGEANT-MAJOR. Very good, sir.

(*He stands back a pace and salutes Stanhope smartly.* STANHOPE's *eye falls on the Sergeant-Major's nearly finished drink on the table. He points to it*)

STANHOPE. Hoy! What about that?

SERGEANT-MAJOR. Thank you, sir. (*He returns to finish the drink*)

(*The* COLONEL *comes down the steps as the* SERGEANT-MAJOR *is drinking:* SERGEANT-MAJOR *puts mug down and makes way for the* COLONEL)

COLONEL. Good morning, Sergeant-Major.

SERGEANT-MAJOR. Good morning, sir.

(*The* SERGEANT-MAJOR *salutes again and exits up the steps*)

STANHOPE. Hullo, sir! (*At the table*)

(*The* COLONEL *comes to* C. STANHOPE *is at the table*)

COLONEL. Hullo, Stanhope! (*He sniffs*) Strong smell of bacon.

STANHOPE. Yes, sir. We had some bacon for breakfast.

COLONEL. Hangs about, doesn't it? (*He looks off into the dug-out* R)

STANHOPE. Yes, sir. Clings to the walls.

COLONEL. Lovely day.

STANHOPE. Splendid, sir.

COLONEL. Spring's coming. (*There is a pause*) I'm glad you're alone. I've got some rather serious news. (*He returns to* C)

STANHOPE. I'm sorry to hear that, sir. Will you have a drink?

COLONEL. Well, thanks—just a spot.

(STANHOPE *pours out a drink, which the* COLONEL *takes, and takes one himself*)

Here's luck.

STANHOPE. Cheero, sir. (*He brings forward a box and places it for the* COLONEL *to sit on* R *of the table.* STANHOPE *then crosses to* L *and sits*) Sit down, sir.

COLONEL. Thanks. (*He puts his tin hat on the ground*)

STANHOPE. What's the news, sir?

COLONEL. The Brigadier came to see me this morning. (*He pauses*) It seems almost certain the attack's to come on Thursday morning. They've got information from more than one source—but they don't know where it's going to fall the hardest. The Boche began relieving his front-line troops yesterday. They're bound to put in certain regiments where they intend to make the hardest push——

STANHOPE. Naturally, sir.

COLONEL. And the General wants us to make a raid to find out who's come into the line opposite here.

(*There is a pause*)

STANHOPE. I see. When?

COLONEL. As soon as possible. He said tonight.

STANHOPE. Oh, but that's absurd, sir!

COLONEL. I told him so. I said the earliest would be tomorrow afternoon. A surprise daylight raid under a smoke-screen from the trench-mortar people. I think daylight best. There's not much moon now, and it's vitally important to get hold of a Boche or two.

STANHOPE. Quite, sir.

COLONEL. I suggest two officers and ten men. Quite enough for the purpose. Just opposite here there's only seventy yards of No-Man's Land. Tonight the trench-mortars can blow a hole in the Boche wire and you can cut a hole in yours. Harrison of the trench-mortars is coming in to dinner with me this evening to discuss everything. I'd like you to come too. Eight o'clock suit you?

STANHOPE. Very good, sir.

COLONEL. I'll leave you to select the men.

STANHOPE. You want me to go with them, sir?

COLONEL. Oh, no, Stanhope. No. I—I can't let you go. No. I want one officer to direct the raid and one to make the dash in and collar some Boche.

STANHOPE. Who do you suggest, sir?

COLONEL. Well, I suggest Osborne, for one. He's a very level-headed chap. He can direct it.

STANHOPE. And who else, sir?

COLONEL. Well, there's Trotter—but he's a bit fat, isn't he? Not much good at dashing in?

STANHOPE. No. D'you suggest Hibbert?

COLONEL. Well, what do *you* think of Hibbert?

STANHOPE. I don't think so.

COLONEL. No.

(*There is a pause*)

STANHOPE. Why not send a good sergeant, sir?

COLONEL. No. I don't think a sergeant. The men expect officers to lead a raid.

STANHOPE. Yes. There is that.

COLONEL. As a matter of fact, Stanhope, I'm thinking of that youngster I sent up to you last night.

STANHOPE. Raleigh, sir?

COLONEL. Yes. Just the type. Plenty of guts——

STANHOPE. He's awfully new to it all——

COLONEL. All to the good. His nerves are sound.

STANHOPE. Isn't it rather rotten to send a fellow who's only just arrived.

COLONEL. Well, who else is there? I could send an officer from another company——

STANHOPE (*quickly*) Oh, Lord, no, sir. We'll do it.

COLONEL. Then I suggest Osborne to direct the raid and Raleigh to make the dash—with ten good men. We'll meet Harrison at supper and arrange the smoke-bombs—and blowing a hole in the wire. You select the men and talk to Osborne and Raleigh about it in the meantime.

STANHOPE. Very well, sir.

COLONEL. Better send Osborne and Raleigh down to me in the morning to talk things over. (*He picks up and puts on his tin hat*) Or, better still!—I'll come up here first thing tomorrow morning.

STANHOPE. Right, sir.

COLONEL. It's all a damn nuisance; but, after all—it's necessary.

STANHOPE. I suppose it is.

COLONEL (*rising and going to the steps*) Well, so long, Stanhope. I'll see you at eight o'clock. (*He pauses and turns*) Do you like fish?

STANHOPE. Fish, sir?

COLONEL. Yes. We've had some fresh fish sent up from rail-head for supper tonight.

STANHOPE (*rising*) Splendid, sir!

COLONEL. Whiting, I think it is.

STANHOPE. Good!

COLONEL. Well, bye-bye.

(*The* COLONEL *goes up the steps and off to* R. STANHOPE *stands watching for a moment, then turns and walks slowly to the table, gets his note-book, sits and writes. After a few seconds* HIBBERT *comes quietly into the dug-out from the tunnel leading from his sleeping quarters off* R)

STANHOPE. Hullo! I thought you were asleep.

HIBBERT. I just wanted a word with you, Stanhope.

STANHOPE. Fire away.

HIBBERT. This neuralgia of mine. I'm awfully sorry. I'm afraid I can't stick it any longer——

STANHOPE. I know. It's rotten, isn't it? I've got it like hell——

HIBBERT (*taken aback*) *You* have?

STANHOPE. Had it for weeks. Aches all day and night.

HIBBERT. Well, I'm sorry, Stanhope. It's no good. I've tried damned hard; but I must go down——

STANHOPE. Go down—where?

HIBBERT. Why, go sick—go down the line. I must go into hospital and have some kind of treatment. I can't bear it any longer.

(*There is a silence for a moment.* STANHOPE *is looking at Hibbert —till* HIBBERT *turns away and walks towards his dug-out*)

I'll go right along now, I think——

STANHOPE (*quietly*) You're going to stay here.

HIBBERT (*stopping and coming back*) I'm going down to see the doctor. He'll send me to hospital when he understands——

STANHOPE. I've seen the doctor. I saw him this morning. He won't send you to hospital, Hibbert; he'll send you back here. He promised me he would. (*There is silence*) So you can save yourself a walk.

HIBBERT (*fiercely*) What the hell——!

STANHOPE. Stop that!

HIBBERT. I've a perfect right to go sick if I want to. The men can—why can't an officer?

STANHOPE. No man's sent down unless he's very ill. There's nothing wrong with you, Hibbert. The German attack's on Thursday; almost for certain. You're going to stay here and see it through with the rest of us.

HIBBERT (*rushing over to Stanhope*) Haven't I told you, I *can't*— the pain's nearly sending me mad. I'm going! I've got all my stuff packed. I'm going now—*you* can't stop me! (*He rushes excitedly into the dug-out*)

(STANHOPE *walks slowly towards the steps, turns, and undoes the flap of his revolver holster. He takes out his revolver, and stands casually examining it, and we hear the click of the trigger.* HIBBERT *returns with his pack slung on his back and a walking-stick in his* R *hand, in his* L *hand his gas mask, etc. He pauses at the sight of Stanhope by the steps, who bars his way*)

Let's get by, Stanhope.

STANHOPE. You're going to stay here and do your job.

HIBBERT. Haven't I *told* you? I *can't*. Don't you understand? Let—let me get by.

STANHOPE. Now look here, Hibbert. I've got a lot of work to do and no time to waste. Once and for all, you're going to stay here and see it through with the rest of us.

HIBBERT. I shall die of this pain if I don't go!

STANHOPE. Better die of the pain than be shot for deserting.

HIBBERT (*in a low voice*) What do you mean?

STANHOPE. You know what I mean——

HIBBERT. I've a right to see the doctor!

STANHOPE. Good God! Don't you understand!—he'll send you back here. Dr Preston's never let a shirker pass him yet—and he's not going to start now—two days before the attack——

HIBBERT (*pleadingly*) Stanhope—if you only *knew* how awful I feel—— Please do let me go by——

(*He walks slowly round behind Stanhope.* STANHOPE *turns and thrusts him roughly back. With a lightning movement* HIBBERT *raises his stick and strikes blindly at* STANHOPE, *who catches the stick, tears it from Hibbert's hands, and throws him on the ground*)

STANHOPE. God!—you bloody little swine. You know what that means—don't you? Striking a superior officer!

(*There is silence.* STANHOPE *takes hold of his revolver as it swings from its lanyard.* HIBBERT *is quivering in front of Stanhope*)

Never mind, though. I won't have you shot for that——

HIBBERT. Let me go——

STANHOPE. If you went, I'd have you shot—for deserting. It's a hell of a disgrace—to die like that. I'd rather spare you the disgrace. I give you half a minute to think. You either stay here and try and be a man—or you try to get out of that door—to desert. If you do that, there's going to be an accident. D'you understand? I'm fiddling with my revolver, d'you see?—cleaning it—and it's going off by accident. It often happens out here. It's going off, and it's going to shoot you between the eyes.

HIBBERT (*in a whisper*) You daren't——

STANHOPE. You don't deserve to be shot by accident—but I'd

save you the disgrace of the other way—I give you half a minute
to decide. (*He holds up his wrist to look at his watch*) Half a minute
from now—

   (*There is silence; a few seconds go by. Suddenly* HIBBERT *bursts
   into a high-pitched laugh*)

HIBBERT (*rising and standing with his back against the wall, arms
outstretched*) Go on, then, shoot! You won't let me go to hospital.
I swear I'll never go into those trenches again. Shoot!—and
thank God——

STANHOPE (*with his eyes on his watch*) Fifteen more seconds——

HIBBERT. Go on! I'm ready——

STANHOPE. Ten. (*He looks up at Hibbert, who has closed his eyes*)
Five.

   (*Again* STANHOPE *looks up. After a moment he quietly drops his
   revolver into its holster and steps towards* HIBBERT, *who stands with
   lowered head and eyes tightly screwed up, his arms stretched stiffly by
   his sides, his hands tightly clutching the edges of his tunic. Gently*
   STANHOPE *places his hands on Hibbert's shoulders.* HIBBERT *starts
   violently and gives a little cry. He opens his eyes and stares vacantly into
   Stanhope's face.* STANHOPE *is smiling*)

STANHOPE. Good man, Hibbert. I liked the way you stuck that.

   (HIBBERT *falls into* STANHOPE'S *arms*)

HIBBERT (*hoarsely*) Why didn't you shoot?

STANHOPE. Stay here, old chap—and see it through—— With
the rest of us.

   (HIBBERT *stands trembling, trying to speak. Suddenly he breaks
   down and cries.* STANHOPE *takes his hands from his shoulders and
   turns away; and* HIBBERT *sinks down on Stanhope's bed* L)

HIBBERT. Stanhope! I've tried like hell—I swear I have. Ever
since I came out here I've hated and loathed it. Every sound up
there makes me all—cold and sick. I'm different to—to the others
—you don't understand. It's got worse and worse, and now I
can't bear it any longer. I'll never go up those steps again—into the
line—with the men looking at me—and knowing—I'd rather die
here. (*He sits on Stanhope's bed crying, without effort to restrain himself*)

STANHOPE (*pouring out a stiff whiskey and handing it to him*) Try
a drop of this, old chap——

HIBBERT. No, thanks.

STANHOPE. Go on. Drink it. (*Rapped out as a command*)

   (HIBBERT *takes the mug, sits up and drinks.* STANHOPE *sits down
   beside Hibbert and puts an arm round his shoulder*)

I know what you feel, Hibbert. I've known all along—— (*He
rises and sits up stage* C *behind the table*)

HIBBERT. How *can* you know?

STANHOPE. Because I feel the same—exactly the same! Every little noise up there makes me feel—just as you feel. Why didn't you tell me instead of talking about neuralgia? We *all* feel like you do sometimes, if you only knew. I hate and loathe it all. Sometimes I feel I could just lie down on this bed and pretend I was paralysed or something—and couldn't move—and just lie there till I died—or was dragged away.

HIBBERT. I can't bear to go up into those awful trenches again——

STANHOPE. When are you due to go on?

HIBBERT. Quite soon. At four.

STANHOPE. Shall we go on together? We know how we both feel now. Shall we see if we can stick it together?

HIBBERT. I can't——

STANHOPE. Supposing I said *I* can't—supposing we *all* say we can't—what would happen then?

HIBBERT. I don't care. What does it matter? It's all so—so beastly—nothing matters——

STANHOPE. Supposing the worst happened—supposing we were knocked right out. Think of all the chaps who've gone already. It can't be very lonely there—with all those fellows. (*Pause*) Sometimes I think it's lonelier here. (*He pauses*)

(HIBBERT *is sitting quietly now, his eyes roving vacantly in front of him*)

Just go and have a quiet rest. Then we'll go out together.

HIBBERT (*rising*) Do please let me go, Stanhope—— (*He grips Stanhope's shoulder*)

STANHOPE. If you went—and left Osborne and Trotter and Raleigh and all those men up there to do your work—could you ever look a man straight in the face again—in all your life? (*He throws him off. There is silence again*) You may be wounded. Then you can go home and feel proud—and if you're killed you—you won't have to stand this hell any more. I might have fired just now. If I had you would have been dead now. But you're still alive—with a straight fighting chance of coming through. Take the chance, old chap, and stand in with Osborne and Trotter and Raleigh. Don't you think it worth standing in with men like that? —when you know they all feel like you do—in their hearts—and just go on sticking it because they know it's—it's the only thing a decent man can do. (*Again there is silence*) Well! What about it?

HIBBERT. I'll—I'll try—— (*He rises and crosses slowly to his dug-out* R)

STANHOPE. Good man!

HIBBERT. You—you won't say anything, Stanhope—about this?

STANHOPE. If you promise not to tell anyone what a blasted funk *I* am.

HIBBERT (*with a little laugh*) No.

STANHOPE. Splendid! Now go and have ten minutes' rest and a smoke—then we'll go up together and hold each other's hands —and jump every time a rat squeaks.

(HIBBERT *blows his nose*)

We've all got a good fighting chance. *I* mean to come through— don't you?

HIBBERT. Yes. Rather. (*He goes timidly towards his dug-out, and turns at the doorway*) It's awfully decent of you, Stanhope—

(STANHOPE *is pouring himself out a whiskey*)

and thanks most awfully for——

STANHOPE. That's all right.

(HIBBERT *goes out* R
    STANHOPE *takes a drink and sits down at the table. He refers to his army book and writes.*
    MASON *has come in from up* L *and stands behind the table in time to notice* HIBBERT's *exit*)

MASON. Will you have a nice cup of tea, sir?

STANHOPE. Can you guarantee it's nice?

MASON. Well, sir—it's a bit oniony, but that's only because of the saucepan.

STANHOPE. In other words, it's onion soup with tea-leaves in it?

MASON. Not till dinner-time, sir.

STANHOPE. All right, Mason. Bring two cups of onion tea. One for Mr Hibbert.

MASON. Very good, sir. (*He goes up, and sees* OSBORNE *coming in*) Will you have a nice cup of tea, sir?

OSBORNE (*crossing round the front of the table and sitting on the bed* L) Please, Mason—and plenty of bread and butter and straw-berry jam.

MASON. Very good, sir.

(MASON *exits*)

STANHOPE. Well, Uncle—how are things going on up there?

OSBORNE. Two lonely rifle grenades came over just now. (*He rises, crosses to* R *and puts his tin hat on bed*)

STANHOPE. I heard them. Where did they pitch?

OSBORNE. Just over the front line on the left. Otherwise nothing doing.

(*Pause*)

STANHOPE. The Colonel's been talking to me.

OSBORNE. About the attack?

STANHOPE. Partly. We've got to make a raid, Uncle.

OSBORNE. Oh? When? (*He starts to take off his belt*)

STANHOPE. Tomorrow afternoon. Under a smoke-screen. Two officers and ten men.

OSBORNE. Who's going?

STANHOPE. You and Raleigh.

(*Pause*)

OSBORNE. Oh. (*There is another pause. He takes off his shoulder strap*) Raleigh?

STANHOPE. Yes. The Colonel picked you to direct and Raleigh to dash in.

OSBORNE. I see.

STANHOPE. The brigade wants to know who's opposite here.

OSBORNE. Tomorrow? What time?

STANHOPE. I suggest about five o'clock. A little before dusk——

OSBORNE. I see. (*He puts his belt on the bed*)

STANHOPE. I'm damn sorry.

OSBORNE. That's all right, old chap.

STANHOPE. I'm dining with the Colonel to arrange everything. Then I'll come back and go through it with you.

OSBORNE. Where do we raid from?

STANHOPE. Out of the sap on our left. Straight across.

OSBORNE. Where's the map?

STANHOPE. Here we are. Look. Straight across to this sentry post of the Boche. Sixty yards. Tonight we'll lay out a guiding tape as far as possible. After dark the toch-emmas are going to break the Boche wire and we'll cut a passage in ours.

OSBORNE. Will you fix up the men who are to go?

STANHOPE. Are you keen on any special men?

OSBORNE. Can I take a corporal!

STANHOPE. Sure.

OSBORNE. May I have young Crooks?

STANHOPE. Righto.

OSBORNE. You'll ask for volunteers, I suppose?

STANHOPE. Yes. I'll see the Sergeant-Major and get him to go round for names. (*He rises, gets his gas mask and tin hat and moves to the step. He crosses to the doorway as* MASON *comes in with the tea*)

MASON. Your tea, sir!

STANHOPE. Keep it hot, Mason.

MASON. Will you take this cup, Mr Osborne?

STANHOPE. Take the other in to Mr Hibbert, in there.

MASON. Very good, sir.

(MASON *goes into Hibbert's dug-out with tea*)

STANHOPE. Shan't be long, Uncle.

(STANHOPE *goes up the steps*)

OSBORNE. Righto. (*He sits above the table*)

(MASON *returns*)

MASON (*above the table*) Will you have cut bread and butter—or shall I bring the loaf, sir?

Osborne. Cut it, Mason, please.
Mason. Just bringing the jam separately?
Osborne. Yes.
Mason. Very good, sir.

(Mason *goes out up* l. Osborne *takes a small leather-bound book from his pocket, opens it at a marker, and begins to read.* Trotter *appears from the sleeping dug-out looking very sleepy*)

Trotter (*stretching himself*) Tea ready?
Osborne. Yes.
Trotter. Why's Hibbert got his tea in there?
Osborne. I don't know.
Trotter (*rubbing his eyes*) Oh, Lord, I do feel frowsy. 'Ad a fine sleep, though.

(Mason *brings more tea and a pot of strawberry jam*)

Mason. Bread just coming, sir. 'Ere's the strawberry jam, sir.
Trotter (*reciting*) ' "Tell me, mother, what is that
                    That looks like strawberry jam?
                    'Hush, hush, my dear; 'tis only Pa
                    Run over by a tram——" '

(*During this* Mason *stares mysteriously at Trotter, and as he finishes* Trotter *sees Mason staring.* Mason *slinks away*)

Osborne. The Colonel came here while you were asleep.
Trotter. Oh?
Osborne. We've got to make a raid tomorrow afternoon.
Trotter. Oh, Lord! What—all of us? (*Pause. He holds his tea, warming his hands*)
Osborne. Two officers and ten men.
Trotter. Who's got to do it?
Osborne. Raleigh and I.
Trotter. Raleigh!
Osborne. Yes.
Trotter. But 'e's only just come!
Osborne. Apparently that's the reason.
Trotter. And you're going too?
Osborne. Yes.
Trotter. Let's 'ear all about it. (*He drinks*)
Osborne. I know nothing yet. Except that it's got to be done.
Trotter. What a damn nuisance!
Osborne. It is, rather.
Trotter. I reckon the Boche will know all about it. Did you 'ear about the raid just south of 'ere the other night?
Osborne. Nothing much.
Trotter. The trench-mortars go and knock an 'ole in the Boche wire to let our fellers through—and in the night the Boche went out and tied bits o' red rag on each side of the 'ole!

OSBORNE. Yes, I heard about that.

TROTTER. And even then our fellers 'ad to make the raid. It was murder. (*He drinks*) This tea tastes of onions?

OSBORNE. It does a bit.

TROTTER. Pity Mason don't clean 'is pots better.

(MASON *brings some bread on a plate and stands behind the table*)

This tea tastes of onions.

MASON. I'm sorry, sir. Onions do 'ave such a way of cropping up again.

TROTTER. Yes, but we 'aven't 'ad onions for days!

MASON. I know, sir. That's what makes it so funny.

TROTTER. Well, you better do something about it.

MASON. Very good, sir, I'll look into it.

(MASON *exits quickly.*

    OSBORNE *and* TROTTER *prepare themselves slices of bread and jam*)

TROTTER. Joking apart. It's damn ridiculous making a raid with the Boche knowing all about it.

OSBORNE. We're not doing it for fun.

TROTTER. I know.

OSBORNE. You might avoid talking to Raleigh about it.

TROTTER. Why? How do you mean? (*He lights a cigarette*)

OSBORNE. There's no need to tell him it's murder——

TROTTER. Oh, Lord! no. (*He pauses*) I'm sorry 'e's got to go. 'E's a nice young feller——

(OSBORNE *turns to his book. There is silence*)

What are you reading?

OSBORNE (*wearily*) Oh, just a book.

TROTTER. What's the title?

OSBORNE (*showing him the cover*) Ever read it?

TROTTER (*getting out his glasses, leaning over and reading the cover*) *Alice's Adventures in Wonderland*—why, that's a kid's book!

OSBORNE. Yes.

TROTTER. You aren't *reading* it?

OSBORNE. Yes.

TROTTER. What—a *kid's* book?

OSBORNE. Haven't you read it?

TROTTER (*scornfully*) No! (*He puts his glasses down*)

OSBORNE. You ought to. (*He reads*)

> 'How doth the little crocodile
> Improve his shining tail,
> And pour the waters of the Nile
> On every golden scale?

How cheerfully he seems to grin
And neatly spread his claws,
And welcomes little fishes in
With gently smiling jaws!'

TROTTER (*after a moment's thought*) I don't see no point in that. (*He drinks his tea*)

OSBORNE (*wearily*) Exactly. That's just the point.

TROTTER (*looking curiously at Osborne*) You *are* a funny chap! (*He puts his cup down*)

(STANHOPE *returns*)

STANHOPE. The Sergeant-Major's getting volunteers.

OSBORNE. Good!

TROTTER. Sorry to 'ear about the raid, skipper.

STANHOPE (*shortly*) So am I. What do you make the time?

TROTTER. Just on four.

(MASON *brings in more tea, puts it on the table and exits*)

STANHOPE (*taking the mug of tea*) Was Hibbert asleep when you came out of there? (*He drinks*)

TROTTER. No. 'E was just lying on 'is bed, smoking.

STANHOPE (*going to the sleeping dug-out*) Hibbert!

HIBBERT (*coming out*) I'm ready, Stanhope. (*He picks up his tin hat from bed*)

STANHOPE. Had some tea?

HIBBERT. Yes, thanks.

TROTTER. I reckon Raleigh'll be glad to be relieved. Rotten being on dooty for the first time alone.

OSBORNE. I don't think he minds.

STANHOPE (*looking at his wrist-watch*) I shall be up there some time, Uncle.

OSBORNE. I say, why don't you have a rest—you've been on the go all day.

STANHOPE. There's too much to do. This raid's going to upset the arrangements of the wiring party tonight. Can't have men out there while the toch-emmas are blowing holes in the Boche wire. (*He drinks up his tea*) Ready, Hibbert? Come on, my lad.

(STANHOPE *and* HIBBERT *exit together,* STANHOPE *first.* TROTTER *looks after them curiously, and turns to Osborne*)

TROTTER. Can't quite make that little blighter out, can you, Uncle?

OSBORNE. Who?

TROTTER. Why, 'Ibbert. D'you see 'is eyes? All red. 'E told me in there 'e'd got 'ay-fever.

OSBORNE. Rotten thing, hay-fever.

TROTTER. If you ask me, 'e's been crying——

(OSBORNE *is writing at the table and rather resents Trotter's interruptions*)

OSBORNE. Maybe.

(TROTTER *rises and forces himself on Osborne by coming* C *and sitting on seat at table, quite close to him*)

TROTTER. Funny little bloke, isn't 'e?

OSBORNE. Yes. I say—d'you mind? I just want to get a letter off.

TROTTER. Oh, sorry. They 'aven't collected the letters yet, then?

OSBORNE. Not yet.

TROTTER. I'll get one off to my old lady. (*He rises and leans against the post* L, *then goes towards his dug-out* R) She's wrote and asked if I've got fleas.

OSBORNE. Have you?

TROTTER (*giving one look at Osborne and gently rotating his shoulders*) I wish it *was* fleas.

(TROTTER *goes into his dug-out;* OSBORNE *resumes his letter, and after a few seconds* RALEIGH *excitedly comes down the steps from the trench, flings his tin hat on the bed* L, *and makes for the table, rests one arm on it, looking into Osborne's face*)

RALEIGH (*excitedly*) I say, Stanhope's told me about the raid.

OSBORNE. Has he?

RALEIGH. Just you and me, isn't it—and ten men?

OSBORNE. Yes, tomorrow. Just before dusk. Under a smoke cloud.

RALEIGH. I say—it's most frightfully exciting.

OSBORNE. We shall know more about it after Stanhope sees the Colonel tonight.

RALEIGH. Were you and I picked—specially?

OSBORNE. Yes.

RALEIGH. I—say! (*He sinks into seat and never takes his eyes off Osborne's face*)

The CURTAIN *falls*

ACT III

SCENE I

SCENE—*The following day, towards sunset. The earth wall of the trench outside glows with a light that slowly fades with the sinking sun.*

STANHOPE is alone, standing C *with his foot on the box* R *of the table. He looks up the steps for a moment, and glances down at the map. He looks anxiously at his watch, and calls:*

STANHOPE (*moving to* L) Mason!
MASON (*outside*) Yessir!
STANHOPE. Are you making the coffee?
MASON. Yessir!
STANHOPE. Make it hot and strong. Ready in five minutes. I'll call when it's wanted.
MASON. Very good, sir.

(STANHOPE *wanders restlessly to and fro until the* COLONEL *comes down the steps and sits on box* R *of the table*)

COLONEL. Everything ready?
STANHOPE. Yes, sir. (*There is silence*) You've no news, then?
COLONEL. I'm afraid not. It's got to be done.
STANHOPE (*after a pause*) I see.
COLONEL. The Brigadier says the Boche did the same thing just south of here the other day.
STANHOPE. I know; but didn't you suggest we altered our plans and made a surprise raid farther up the line after dark?
COLONEL. Yes. I suggested that.
STANHOPE. What did he say?
COLONEL. He said the present arrangements have got to stand.
STANHOPE. But surely he must realize——?
COLONEL (*impatiently breaking in*) Look here, Stanhope, I've done all I can, but my report's got to be at headquarters by seven this evening. If we wait till it's dark we shall be too late.
STANHOPE. Why seven? (*He moves to the table and sits*)
COLONEL. They've got some conference to arrange the placing of reserves.
STANHOPE. They can't have it later because of dinner, I suppose.
COLONEL. Nonsense! With the attack tomorrow morning, headquarters naturally want all the information they can get as early as possible.
STANHOPE. Meanwhile the Boche are sitting over there with a dozen machine-guns trained on that hole—waiting for our fellows to come.
COLONEL. Well, I can't disobey orders.

54

STANHOPE. Why didn't the trench-mortars blow a dozen holes in different places—so that the Boche wouldn't know which we were going to use?

COLONEL. It took three hours to blow that one. How could they blow a dozen in the time? It's no good worrying about that now. It's too late. Where's Osborne and Raleigh?

STANHOPE. They're up in the sap, having a last look round. What d'you make the time, sir?

COLONEL. Exactly nineteen minutes to.

STANHOPE. I'm thirty seconds behind you.

COLONEL. Funny. We checked this morning.

STANHOPE. Still, it's near enough. We shan't go till the smoke blows across.

COLONEL. The smoke ought to blow across nicely. The wind's just right. I called on the trench-mortars on the way up. Everything's ready. They'll drop the bombs thirty yards to the right.

STANHOPE. Are you going to stay here?

COLONEL. I'll watch from the trench just above, I think. Bring the prisoners straight back here. We'll question them right away.

STANHOPE. Why not take them straight down to your headquarters, sir?

COLONEL. Well, the Boche are bound to shell pretty heavily. I don't want the risk of the prisoners being knocked out before we've talked to them.

STANHOPE. All right. I'll have them brought back here. (*He rises*)

(*There is a pause. The* COLONEL *sucks hard at his pipe.* STANHOPE *roves restlessly to* R, *smoking a cigarette*)

COLONEL. It's no good getting depressed. (*He refers to his notebook, which is open on the table*) After all, it's only sixty yards. The Boche'll be firing into a blank fog. Osborne's a cool, level-headed chap, and Raleigh's the very man to dash in. You've picked good men to follow them?

STANHOPE. The best. All youngsters. Strong, keen chaps. (*He moves across to the seat above the table and sits*)

COLONEL. Good. (*Another pause*) You know quite well I'd give anything to cancel the beastly affair.

STANHOPE. I know you would, sir.

COLONEL. Have these red rags on the wire upset the men at all?

STANHOPE. It's hard to tell. They naturally take it as a joke. They say the rags are just what they want to show them the way through the gap.

COLONEL. That's the spirit, Stanhope.

(OSBORNE, *followed by* RALEIGH, *come down the steps and stand down stage* RC)

Well, Osborne. Everything ready?

Osborne. Yes, I think we're all ready, sir. I make it just a quarter to.

Colonel. That's right.

Osborne. The men are going to stand by at three minutes to.

Colonel. The smoke-bombs drop exactly on the hour! You'll give the word to go when the smoke's thick enough?

Osborne (*crossing in front to* L *of the table*) That's right, sir.

(Raleigh *puts his hat on the bed* R)

Stanhope (*at the servant's dug-out*) Mason!

Mason. Coming, sir!

Stanhope. Were the men having their rum, Uncle?

Osborne. Yes. Just as we left. It gives it a quarter of an hour to soak in.

Colonel. That's right. Are they cheerful?

Osborne. Yes. Quite.

(Mason *brings in two cups of coffee and puts them on the table*)

Stanhope. Would you like to go up and speak to them, sir?

Colonel. Well, don't you think they'd rather be left alone?

Stanhope. I think they would appreciate a word or two.

Colonel. All right. If you think they would.

Osborne. They're all in the centre dug-out, sir.

Colonel. Right. You coming, Stanhope? (*He rises and moves* c. *Pause*)

Stanhope. Yes. I'll come, sir.

(*The* Colonel *lingers a moment. There is an awkward pause. Then the* Colonel *clears his throat and speaks as he comes to* LC, *holding out his hand*)

Colonel. Well, good luck, Osborne. I'm certain you'll put up a good show.

Osborne (*taking the Colonel's hand*) Thank you, sir.

(*The* Colonel *moves back to* Raleigh *and offers his hand, which* Raleigh *takes*)

Colonel. And, Raleigh, just go in like blazes. Grab hold of the first Boche you see and bundle him across here. One'll do, but bring more if you see any handy.

Raleigh (*taking the Colonel's offered hand*) Right, sir.

Colonel. And, if you succeed, I'll recommend you both for the M.C.

(Osborne *and* Raleigh *murmur their thanks*)

Remember, a great deal may depend on bringing in a German. It may mean the winning of the whole war. You never know. (*Another pause*) Well, good luck to you both.

(*Again* OSBORNE *and* RALEIGH *murmur their thanks. The*
COLONEL *and* STANHOPE *go towards the steps*)

(*He speaks over his shoulder two or three steps up*) Don't forget to
empty your pockets of papers and things.

RALEIGH. Oh, no. (*He goes off into his dug-out* R, *taking letters and
papers from his pockets*)

(STANHOPE *is about to follow the Colonel up the steps when*
OSBORNE *calls him back*)

OSBORNE. Er—Stanhope—just a moment.

STANHOPE (*returning*) Hullo!

OSBORNE. I say, don't think I'm being morbid, or anything like
that, but would you mind taking care of these for me?

STANHOPE. Sure. Until you come back, old man.

OSBORNE. It's only just in case—— (*He takes a letter and his
watch from his tunic pocket and puts them on the table. Then he pulls off
his ring, which must appear to fit tightly, and puts it on the table*) If anything should happen, would you send these along to my wife?
(*He pauses, and gives an awkward little laugh*)

STANHOPE (*putting the articles together on the table*) You're coming
back, old man. Damn it! what on earth should I do without you?
(*He puts his hands on Osborne's arms*)

OSBORNE (*facing him and laughing*) Goodness knows!

STANHOPE. Must have somebody to tuck me up in bed. (*There
is a pause*) Well, I'll see you in the sap, before you go. Just have
a spot of rum in that coffee.

OSBORNE. Righto.

(STANHOPE *goes to the steps and lingers for a moment, giving him a
farewell look*)

STANHOPE. Cheero!

(*For a second their eyes meet; they laugh.* STANHOPE *goes slowly up
the steps. There is silence in the dug-out.* OSBORNE *has been filling his
pipe, and stands lighting it as* RALEIGH *returns*)

OSBORNE. Just time for a small pipe.

RALEIGH. Good. I'll have a cigarette, I think. (*He feels in his
pocket*)

OSBORNE. Have one of mine. (*Offering his case to Raleigh*)

(RALEIGH *is standing* RC. OSBORNE *comes to him and offers him a
cigarette which he takes and lights with candle brought by* OSBORNE)

RALEIGH. I say, I'm always smoking yours.

OSBORNE. That's all right.

(*Pause.* OSBORNE *returns to his seat* L *of the table and* RALEIGH *sits*
R *of the table*)

What about this coffee?

RALEIGH. Sure.

OSBORNE. Are you going to have a drop of rum in it?

RALEIGH. Don't you think it might make us a—a bit muzzy?

OSBORNE. I'm just having the coffee as it is.

RALEIGH. I think I will, too.

OSBORNE. We'll have the rum afterwards—to celebrate.

RALEIGH. That's a much better idea. (*He sips his coffee*)

(*They stir their coffee in silence.* OSBORNE'S *eyes meet* RALEIGH'S. *He smiles*)

OSBORNE. How d'you feel?

RALEIGH. All right. (*He drinks. Long pause*)

OSBORNE. I've got a sort of empty feeling inside.

RALEIGH. That's just what I've got!

OSBORNE. Wind up!

RALEIGH. I keep wanting to yawn.

OSBORNE. That's it. Wind up. I keep wanting to yawn too. It'll pass off directly we start.

RALEIGH (*taking a deep breath*) I wish we could go now. (*He turns and looks outside*)

OSBORNE (*looking at his watch on the table*) We've got eight minutes yet.

RALEIGH. Oh, Lord!

OSBORNE (*rising*) Let's just have a last look at the map. (*He picks up the map and spreads it out*)

(RALEIGH *rises and crosses in front of the table to Osborne and holds the candle*)

Directly the smoke's thick enough, I'll give the word. You run straight for this point here——

RALEIGH. When I get to the Boche wire I lie down and wait for you.

OSBORNE. Don't forget to throw your bombs.

RALEIGH (*patting his pocket*) No. I've got them here.

OSBORNE. When I shout 'Righto!'—in you go with your eight men. I shall lie on the Boche parapet, and blow my whistle now and then to show you where I am. Pounce on the first Boche you see and bundle him out to me. (*He sits* L *of the table*)

RALEIGH. Righto. (*He returns to his seat* R *of the table and puts down the candle*)

OSBORNE. Then we come back like blazes.

RALEIGH. The whole thing'll be over quite quickly?

OSBORNE. I reckon with luck we shall be back in three minutes.

RALEIGH. As quick as that?

OSBORNE. I think so. (*He folds up the map*) And now let's forget all about it for—(*he looks at his watch*)—for six minutes.

RALEIGH. Oh, Lord, I can't!

OSBORNE. You must.

RALEIGH. How topping if we both get the M.C.!

OSBORNE. Yes. (*Pause. They drink*) Your coffee sweet enough?

RALEIGH. Yes, thanks. It's jolly good coffee. (*Pause. He looks up the steps to outside*) I wonder what the Boche are doing over there now?

OSBORNE. I don't know. D'you like coffee better than tea?

RALEIGH. I do for breakfast. (*Pause*) Do those smoke-bombs make much row when they burst?

OSBORNE. Not much. (*Pause. He looks into his mug*) Personally, I like cocoa for breakfast.

RALEIGH (*laughing*) I'm sorry!

OSBORNE. Why sorry? Why shouldn't I have cocoa for breakfast?

RALEIGH. I don't mean that. I—mean—I'm sorry to keep talking about the raid. It's so difficult to—to talk about anything else. I was just wondering—will the Boche retaliate in any way after the raid?

OSBORNE. Bound to—a bit.

RALEIGH. Shelling?

OSBORNE (*putting down his mug*) ' "The time has come," the Walrus said,
"To talk of many things:
Of shoes—and ships—and sealing-wax—
Of cabbages—and kings." '

RALEIGH. ' "And why the sea is boiling hot—
And whether pigs have wings." '

OSBORNE. Now we're off! Quick, let's talk about pigs! Black pigs or white pigs?

(*Electrics Cue* 1)

RALEIGH. Black pigs. In the New Forest you find them, quite wild.

OSBORNE. You know the New Forest?

RALEIGH. Rather! My home's down there. A little place called Allum Green, just outside Lyndhurst.

OSBORNE. I know Lyndhurst well.

RALEIGH. It's rather nice down there.

OSBORNE. I like it more than any place I know. (*He lights his pipe*)

RALEIGH. I think I do, too. Of course, it's different when you've always lived in a place.

OSBORNE. You like it in a different way.

RALEIGH. Yes. Just behind our house there's a stream called the Highland; it runs for miles—right through the middle of the forest. Dennis and I followed it once as far as we could.

OSBORNE. I used to walk a lot round Lyndhurst.

RALEIGH. I wish we'd known each other then. You could have come with Dennis and me.

OSBORNE. I wish I had. I used to walk alone.

RALEIGH. You must come and stay with us one day.

OSBORNE. I should like to—awfully.

RALEIGH. I can show you places in the forest that nobody knows about except Dennis and me. It gets thicker and darker and cooler, and you stir up all kinds of funny wild animals.

OSBORNE. They say there are ruins, somewhere in the forest, of villages that William the Conqueror pulled down to let the forest grow.

RALEIGH. I know. We often used to look for them, but we haven't found them yet. (*Pause*) You must come and help look one day.

OSBORNE. I'll find them all right.

RALEIGH. Then you can write to the papers. 'Dramatic Discovery of Professor Osborne!'

(OSBORNE *laughs*)

OSBORNE. I did go exploring once—digging up Roman remains.

RALEIGH. Did you find anything?

OSBORNE. We found a horseshoe—and a Roman penny.

RALEIGH (*laughing*) Splendid!

OSBORNE. It's awfully fascinating, digging like that.

RALEIGH. It must be.

(OSBORNE *glances at his watch*)

Is it time yet?

OSBORNE. Two minutes. Then we must go up. I wish we had a good hot bath waiting for us when we get back.

RALEIGH. So do I. (*Pause*) We're having something special for dinner, aren't we?

OSBORNE. How did you know? It's supposed to be a secret.

RALEIGH. Mason dropped a hint.

OSBORNE. Well, we've had a fresh chicken sent up from Noyelle Farm.

RALEIGH. I say!

OSBORNE. And a most awful luxury—two bottles of champagne and half a dozen cigars! One each, and one spare one in case one explodes.

RALEIGH. I've never smoked a cigar.

OSBORNE. It's bound to make you sick.

(RALEIGH *notices Osborne's ring on the table; he picks it up*)

RALEIGH. I say, here's your ring.

OSBORNE. Yes. I'm—I'm leaving it here. I don't want the risk of losing it. (OSBORNE *does not look at Raleigh*)

RALEIGH. Oh! (*There is silence. He puts the ring slowly down, we hear it clatter on the table*)

OSBORNE (*rising*) Well, I think perhaps we ought to get ready

RALEIGH. Yes. Righto. (*He also rises* RC)

OSBORNE. I'm not going to wear a belt—just my revolver, with the lanyard round my neck.

RALEIGH. I see. (*He puts his lanyard round his neck and grips his revolver*) I feel better with this in my hand, don't you?

OSBORNE. Yes. Something to hold. Loaded all right?

RALEIGH. Yes.

(*They put on their helmets.* OSBORNE *takes his pipe from his mouth, fondles it lovingly, and lays it carefully on the table*)

OSBORNE. I do hate leaving a pipe when it's got a nice glow on the top like that.

RALEIGH (*with a short laugh*) What a pity!

(*Electric Cue* I *finishes here.*
    There is another pause. OSBORNE *glances at his watch as it lies on the table*)

OSBORNE. Three minutes to. I think we'd better go.

RALEIGH. Righto.

(*Their eyes meet as* OSBORNE *turns from the table*)

OSBORNE (*coming to him and resting one foot on the box*) I'm glad it's you and I—together, Raleigh.

RALEIGH (*eagerly*) Are you—really?

OSBORNE. Yes.

RALEIGH. So am I—awfully.

OSBORNE. We must put up a good show.

RALEIGH. Yes. Rather!

(*There is a short pause*)

OSBORNE. Let's go along, shall we?

RALEIGH. Righto.

(*They both go out to the trench above,* OSBORNE *first.*
    MASON *comes to the entrance of his dug-out as they reach the top*)

MASON. Good luck, sir.

OSBORNE. Thanks, Mason.

MASON. Good luck, Mr. Raleigh.

RALEIGH. Thanks.

(OSBORNE *and* RALEIGH *disappear together into the pale evening sun.* MASON *tidies the papers on the table; picks up the two coffee-mugs, gives a look of disgust as the raid starts, then exits.*
    There is silence in the trenches above the deserted dug-out. Then, suddenly, there comes the dull 'crush' of bursting smoke-bombs, followed in a second by the vicious rattle of machine-guns. (Electrics Cue 2 *continued for thirty seconds till six maroons. Machine-guns fire. Electrics —one magnesium flash followed by one maroon.) The red and green*

glow of German alarm rockets comes faintly through the dug-out door. Then comes the thin whistle and crash of falling shells; first one by itself, then two, almost together. Quicker and quicker they come, till the noise mingles together in confused turmoil. Yet the noise is deadened by the earth walls of the tiny dug-out, and comes quite softly till the whine of one shell rises above the others to a shriek and a crash. A dark funnel of earth leaps up beyond the parapet of the trench outside; earth falls and rattles down the steps, and a black cloud of smoke rises slowly out of sight. Gradually the noise dies away—there is a longer pause between the crash of each bursting shell. The machine-guns stop—rattle again and stop—rattle for the last time—and stop. Voices are calling in the trench outside; STANHOPE's voice is heard)

STANHOPE. All right, sir. Come down quickly!
COLONEL. How many?

(Electrics—1 maroon here. Cue 3. Go)

STANHOPE. Only one.

(Another shell whines and shrieks and crashes near by. There is silence for a moment, then STANHOPE speaks again)

Hurt, sir?
COLONEL. No. It's all right.

(STANHOPE, pale and haggard, comes down the steps, followed by the COLONEL, who sits at R of the table)

STANHOPE *(calling up the steps)* Bring him down, Sergeant-Major.
SERGEANT-MAJOR *(above)* Coming, sir.
STANHOPE *(to the Colonel)* You won't want me, will you?
COLONEL. Well—er——
STANHOPE. I want to go and see those men.
COLONEL. Oh, all right.

(STANHOPE goes to the door, making way for the SERGEANT-MAJOR to come down, followed by a bareheaded GERMAN BOY, in field grey, sobbing bitterly. Behind come two SOLDIERS with fixed bayonets, who stand R and L of the entrance. STANHOPE exits up the steps. The SERGEANT-MAJOR takes the GERMAN BOY by the arm and draws him into the C of the dug-out to face the COLONEL, who has seated himself at the table. The two SOLDIERS stand behind)

SERGEANT-MAJOR *(soothingly to the German Boy)* All right, sonny, we 'ain't going to 'urt you.

(Suddenly the Boy falls on his knees and sobs out some words in broken English)

GERMAN (RC). Mercy—mister—mercy!
SERGEANT-MAJOR *(on his L)* Come on, lad, get up.

(With a huge fist he takes the Boy by the collar and draws him to his feet. The prisoner stands rigidly to attention. The Boy sobs hysterically. The Colonel clears his throat and begins in somewhat poor German)

Colonel. Was ist sein Regiment?

German. Wurtembergisches.

(The Colonel writes his answers in his book)

Colonel. Was ist der nummer von sein Regiment?

German. Zwanzig.

Colonel *(making a note)* Twentieth Wurtembergers. *(He looks up again)* Wann kommen sie hier?

German. Gestern Abend.

Colonel *(making a note and looking up again)* Wo kommen sie hier?

German *(after a moment's thought)* Mein Geburtsort?

Colonel *(forgetting himself for a moment)* What's that?

German *(in halting English)* You—wish—to—know—where I was—born?

Colonel. No! What town did you come up to the line from?

German *(after a little hesitation, looking away from the Colonel, staring in front)* I—do not tell you.

Colonel. Oh, well, that's all right. *(To the Sergeant-Major)* Search him.

(The Sergeant-Major picks up the Boy's hands, raises them above his head and searches him. He produces a small book)

Sergeant-Major. Looks like 'is pay-book, sir. *(He hands it to the Colonel)*

Colonel *(looking eagerly into the book)* Good.

(The Sergeant-Major discovers a packet of letters; the German Boy clutches it impulsively)

Sergeant-Major. 'Ere, stop that!

German. Lassen sie mich! *(He pauses)* Let—me—please—keep —that.

Sergeant-Major *(very embarrassed)* You let go! *(He wrenches the packet away and gives it to the Colonel)*

Colonel *(glancing at the packet)* Look like letters. May be useful. Is that all, Sergeant-Major?

Sergeant-Major *(looking at a few articles in his hands)* 'Ere's a few oddments, sir—bit o' string, sir; little box o' fruit drops; pocket-knife, sir; bit o' cedar pencil—and a stick o' chocolate, sir.

Colonel. Let him have those back, except the pocket-knife.

Sergeant-Major. Very good, sir. *(He turns to the German Boy with a smile)* 'Ere you are, sonny.

(He returns the oddments, which the German Boy takes back. The Sergeant-Major places the pocket-knife on the table)

COLONEL. All right, Sergeant-Major. Send him straight back to my headquarters. I'll question him again there.

SERGEANT-MAJOR. Very good, sir. (*He turns to the German*) Come on, sonny, up you go. (*He points up the steps*)

(*The* GERMAN BOY, *calm now, clicks his heels smartly, bows stiffly to the Colonel and goes away, followed by the two* SOLDIERS *and the* SERGEANT-MAJOR. *The* COLONEL *is deeply absorbed in the German's pay-book. He mutters* 'Splendid' *to himself, then looks at his watch and rises quickly.*

STANHOPE *comes slowly down the steps to* L *of the table. He is covered with dust*)

COLONEL (*excitedly*) Splendid, Stanhope! We've got all we wanted—20th Wurtembergers! His regiment came into the line last night. I must go right away and 'phone the Brigadier. He'll be very pleased about it. It's a feather in our cap, Stanhope. (*He collects the papers*)

(STANHOPE *has given one look of astonishment at the Colonel and strolled past him. He turns at the table and speaks in a dead voice*)

STANHOPE (*bitterly*) How awfully nice—if the Brigadier's pleased.

(*The* COLONEL *stares at Stanhope and suddenly collects himself*)

COLONEL (*rising and moving slightly to* RC) Oh—er—what about the raiding-party—are they all safely back?

STANHOPE. Did you expect them to be all safely back, sir?

COLONEL. Oh—er—what—er——

STANHOPE. Four men and Raleigh came safely back, sir.

COLONEL. Oh, I say, I'm sorry! That's—er—six men and—er —Osborne?

STANHOPE. Yes, sir.

COLONEL. I'm very sorry. Poor Osborne!

STANHOPE. Still, it'll be awfully nice if the Brigadier's pleased.

COLONEL. Don't be silly, Stanhope. Do you know—er—what happened to Osborne?

STANHOPE. A hand grenade—while he was waiting for Raleigh.

COLONEL. I'm very sorry. And the six men?

(RALEIGH *appears at the top of the steps. Comes slowly down*)

STANHOPE. Machine-gun bullets, I suppose.

COLONEL. Yes. I was afraid—er——

(*His words trail away; he fidgets uneasily as* STANHOPE *looks at him with a pale, expressionless face. The* COLONEL, *to the boy, with enthusiasm*)

Very well done, Raleigh. Well done, my boy. I'll get you a Military Cross for this! Splendid!

(RALEIGH *looks at the Colonel, and tries to speak. He raises his hand to his forehead and sways. The* COLONEL *takes him by the arm and helps him*)

Sit down here, my boy.

(RALEIGH *sits on the edge of Osborne's bed* R)

Have a good rest. Well, I must be off. (*He moves towards the steps, and, turning once more to Raleigh as he leaves*) Very well done.

(*The* COLONEL *exits quickly up the steps.*
     There is silence now in the trenches outside; the last shell has whistled over and crashed. Dusk is beginning to fall over the German lines. The glow of 'Verey' lights begins to rise and fade against the evening sky. STANHOPE *is staring dumbly at the table—at Osborne's watch and ring. Presently he turns his haggard face towards* RALEIGH, *who sits with lowered head, looking at the palms of his hands, which are bleeding.* STANHOPE *moves slowly across towards the doorway, and pauses to look down at Raleigh.* RALEIGH *looks up into Stanhope's face, and their eyes meet. When* STANHOPE *speaks, his voice is still expressionless and dead*)

STANHOPE. Must you sit on Osborne's bed?

(*He turns and goes slowly up the steps and exits.*
     RALEIGH *tries to rise by clutching the post with his* L *hand, murmurs 'Sorry' and stands with lowered head. He is still doubled up and broken as the* CURTAIN *falls. Heavy guns are booming miles away*)

The CURTAIN *falls*

SCENE 2

SCENE—*Late evening on the same day.*
     The dug-out is lit quite festively by an unusual number of candles. Two champagne bottles stand prominent on the table. Dinner is over.
     STANHOPE, *seated behind the table* C, *with a cigar between his teeth, lounges across the table, one elbow among the plates and mugs. His hair is ruffled; there is a bright red flush on his cheeks. He has just made a remark which has sent* HIBBERT *and* TROTTER *into uproarious laughter; he listens with a smile.* TROTTER *is sitting on the box to the right of the table, leaning back against the post. A cigar is embedded in his podgy fingers; his face is a shiny scarlet, with deep red patches below the ears. The three bottom buttons of his tunic are undone, and now and then his hand steals gently over his distended stomach.* HIBBERT *sits on the bed to the left, his thin white fingers nervously twitching the ash from his cigar. His pale face is shiny with sweat from the heat of the candles; his laugh is high-pitched and excited.* TROTTER *speaks in a husky voice as the laughter dies away.*

TROTTER (*to Stanhope*) And what did she say to that?

STANHOPE. She said, 'Not in these trousers'—in French.

(TROTTER *and* HIBBERT *burst into laughter again*)

TROTTER (*coughing and wheezing*) Oh—dear-o-dear!

STANHOPE. I simply drew myself up and said, 'Very well, mam'sel, have it your own way.'

TROTTER. And she did?

STANHOPE. No. She didn't.

(*Again the others laugh.* TROTTER *wipes a tear from his eye*)

TROTTER. Oh, skipper, you *are* a scream—and no mistake!

HIBBERT. I never forget picking up a couple of tarts one night and taking 'em out to dinner.

TROTTER (*winking at Stanhope*) 'E's orf again.

HIBBERT. We drank enough bubbly to sink a battleship——

STANHOPE. To *float* a battleship.

HIBBERT. Well—to float a battleship. Then I took 'em for a joy-ride out to Maidenhead—did sixty all the way. We danced a bit at Skindles, and drank a lot of port and muck. Then damned if I didn't lose the way coming back—got landed miles from anywhere. And those tarts began cursing me like hell—said I'd done it on purpose. I said if they didn't damn well shut up, I'd chuck 'em both out in the road and leave 'em.

STANHOPE (*ironically*) Hurrah! That's the stuff! Treat 'em rough!

HIBBERT (*giggling*) That shut 'em up all right! Then I started doing about sixty down all sorts of roads—I went round a corner on two wheels with those girls' hair on end—didn't have any more trouble from *them*! (*He chuckles at the memory, and takes an unsteady gulp of champagne*)

STANHOPE. You're the sort of man who makes girls hard to please.

TROTTER (*heavily*) Well, I never 'ad no motor-car; my old lady and me used to walk; legs is good enough for me.

STANHOPE. You satisfied with legs?

TROTTER. *I* am—yes!

STANHOPE. Much cheaper.

HIBBERT (*laughing delightedly*) That's damn good!

STANHOPE (*raising his mug*) Well, here's a toast to legs—God bless 'em!

HIBBERT (*raising his mug*) Good old legs!

TROTTER (*raising his mug*) Shanks's mare.

STANHOPE. Shanks's *what*?

TROTTER. Shanks's mare they call 'em.

STANHOPE. Call what?

TROTTER. Why—legs.

HIBBERT (*almost screaming with delight*) Oh, Trotter! you're a dream!

TROTTER (*turning a baleful eye on Hibbert*). You've 'ad too much champagne, you 'ave.

(HIBBERT *takes a leather case from his pocket and produces four picture post-cards.*)

HIBBERT. I say, I've never shown you these, have I?

(*He hands them one by one to* STANHOPE, *smiling up into Stanhope's face for approval*)

STANHOPE. Where did you get these from?

HIBBERT. In Bethune. (*He hands up a card*) She's all right, isn't she?

STANHOPE. Too fat.

HIBBERT (*looking over Stanhope's shoulder*) Oh, I don't know.

STANHOPE. Much too fat. (*He hands the card to* TROTTER) What do you think, Trotter?

(TROTTER *takes a pair of pince-nez from his pocket, balances them on his fat nose, and looks at the picture*)

HIBBERT. All right, isn't she?

TROTTER. Well, I don't know. If you ask me, I'd just as soon see a decent picture of Margate Pier.

HIBBERT (*impatiently*) Oh, you don't understand *art*. (*He hands another card to* STANHOPE) There's a nice pair of legs for you.

STANHOPE. Too thin—aren't they, Trotter? (*He hands* TROTTER *the card*)

TROTTER (*after some thought*) Scraggy, I call 'em.

HIBBERT (*handing* STANHOPE *another card*) *That's* the one I like best.

STANHOPE. Not bad.

HIBBERT. Glorious bedroom eyes.

STANHOPE. She's all right.

HIBBERT. Ever see that show *Zip* at the Hippodrome? Couple of damn fine girls in that—twins. Did you see 'em, skipper?

STANHOPE (*wearily*). I don't know—seen stacks of shows—can't remember them all. (*He brightens up*) Now then, swallow up that bubbly! Hi! Mason!

MASON. Yessir!

(MASON *comes just inside the opening*)

STANHOPE. Bring some whiskey.

MASON. Yessir.

(*He disappears again*)

TROTTER. What? Whiskey on top of champagne?

STANHOPE. Why not? It's all right.

TROTTER. Well, I don't know; doesn't sound right to me. I feel as if somebody's blown me up with a bicycle pump.

STANHOPE. You look it, too.

TROTTER (*blowing a stream of cigar smoke up to the dark ceiling*)
Any'ow, it was a jolly fine bit o' chicken—and I'd go a mile any
day for a chunk o' that jam pudding.

(MASON *brings a bottle of whiskey, and puts it on the table*)

STANHOPE. Your pudding's made Mr Trotter feel all blown out,
Mason.

MASON (*standing behind table*) I'm sorry, sir; it wasn't meant, sir.

TROTTER. It was all right, Mason, take it from me. I know a
decent bit o' pudden when I see it.

MASON. It was only boiled ration biscuits and jam, sir. (*He turns
to Stanhpe*) I thought I better tell you, sir—this is the last
bottle.

STANHOPE. The last bottle! Why, damn it, we brought six!

MASON. I know, sir. But five's gone.

STANHOPE. Where the devil's it gone to?

MASON. Well, sir, you remember there was one on the first
night—and then one——

STANHOPE. Oh, for Lord's sake don't go through them one by
one; this'll last till sunrise. (*Turning to Trotter and Hibbert*)
Sunrise tomorrow, my lads!

TROTTER. Oh, forget that.

STANHOPE. You bet we will! Now then! Who's for a spot of
whiskey?

TROTTER. I reckon I'm about full up. I'd like a nice cup o' tea,
Mason.

MASON. Very good, sir.

(*He goes out*)

STANHOPE. Tea!

TROTTER. Yes. That's what I want. Decent cup o' tea. Still,
I'll just 'ave about a spoonful o' whiskey. Just to settle the vittals.
Got a touch of pulpitations.

STANHOPE. Here you are—say when!

TROTTER. Wo! That's enough!

STANHOPE. You'll have a decent spot, won't you, Hibbert!

HIBBERT. Yes. I'm game!

TROTTER (*stifling a hiccup*) Just a cup o' tea—then I'll go and
relieve young Raleigh. Pity 'e didn't come down to supper.

STANHOPE. I told him to. I told him to come down for an hour
and let the Sergeant-Major take over.

TROTTER. I wonder why 'e didn't come.

HIBBERT. That lad's too keen on his 'duty'. He told me he liked
being up there with the men better than down here with us.

STANHOPE (*quietly*) He said that?

HIBBERT. Yes. I told him about the chicken and champagne
and cigars—and he stared at me and said, 'You're not having

that, are you?'—just as if he thought we were going to chuck it
away!

TROTTER. I reckon that raid shook 'im up more'n we thought.
I like that youngster. 'E's got pluck. Strong lad, too—the way
he came back through the smoke after that raid, carrying that
Boche under 'is arm like a baby.

HIBBERT. Did you see him afterwards, though? He came into
that dug-out there, staring straight in front of him, and never said
a word—didn't seem to know where he was.

TROTTER. Well, 'e's only a lad.

STANHOPE (to Hibbert). He actually told you he preferred being
up with the men better than down here?

HIBBERT. That's what he said.

TROTTER. Well, I 'ope 'e gets the M.C., that's all; 'e's just the
kid I'd like if ever I 'ave a kid—strong and plucky.

STANHOPE. Oh, for God's sake forget that bloody raid! Think
I want to talk about it?

TROTTER (surprised) No—but, after all——

STANHOPE. Well—shut up!

TROTTER (uneasily) All right—all right.

STANHOPE. We were having a jolly decent evening till you
started blabbing about the war.

TROTTER. I didn't start it.

STANHOPE. You did.

TROTTER. You began it about——

STANHOPE. Well, for God's sake stop it, then!

TROTTER. All right—all right.

HIBBERT (on the bed L, his feet up stage) Did I ever tell you the
story about the girl I met in Soho?

STANHOPE. I don't know—I expect you did.

HIBBERT (undismayed) It'll amuse you. I'd been to a dance, and
I was coming home quite late——

STANHOPE. Yes, and it's late now. You go on duty at eleven.
You better go and get some sleep.

HIBBERT. It's all right. I'm as fresh as a daisy.

STANHOPE. You may be. But go to bed.

HIBBERT. What?

STANHOPE (louder) I said, 'Go to bed!'

HIBBERT. I say, that's a nice end to a jolly evening!

STANHOPE. I'm sorry. I'm tired.

HIBBERT (perkily, putting his hand on Stanhope's shoulder. STAN-
HOPE resents it and brushes it off angrily) Well, you better go to bed!

(There is silence. STANHOPE looks at HIBBERT, who sniggers)

STANHOPE. What was that you said?

HIBBERT. I was only joking.

STANHOPE. I asked you what you said.

HIBBERT. I said, 'You better go to bed.'

(STANHOPE'S *flushed face is looking full into Hibbert's.* HIBBERT *gives the ghost of a snigger*)

STANHOPE. Clear out of here!

HIBBERT (*rising unsteadily, leaning on the table*) What—what d'you mean?

STANHOPE. Get out of here, for God's sake!

HIBBERT (*blustering*) I say—look here——

STANHOPE. Get out of my sight!

(*With a frightened glance at Stanhope,* HIBBERT *sneaks quietly away into his dug-out.*

There is silence, and the guns can be heard—deep and ominous)

Little worm gets on my nerves.

TROTTER. Poor little bloke. Never seen 'im so cheerful before out 'ere.

STANHOPE. Doesn't he nearly drive you mad?

TROTTER. I reckon 'e only wanted to keep cheerful.

STANHOPE. Doesn't his repulsive little mind make you *sick*?

(MASON *brings Trotter's mug of tea, which he puts on the table* L *of Trotter and exits*)

I envy you, Trotter. Nothing upsets you, does it? You're always the same.

TROTTER. Always the same, am I? (*He sighs*) Little you know——

STANHOPE. You never get sick to death of everything, or so happy you want to sing.

TROTTER. I don't know—I whistle sometimes.

STANHOPE. But you always *feel* the same.

TROTTER. I feel all blown out now.

(*There is a pause.* TROTTER *sips his tea and* STANHOPE *takes a whiskey*)

'Ere's 'Ibbert's post-cards. Funny a bloke carrying pictures like this about. Satisfies 'is lust, I s'pose—poor little blighter. (*He rises, gets his kit on and carefully puts the post-cards into his breast pocket*) Well, I'll go and relieve young Raleigh. Pity 'e didn't come down to supper. (*He tries to button his tunic, without success. He buckles his webbing belt over his unbuttoned tunic, puts on his helmet, and slings his respirator over his shoulder*) Well, cheero!

STANHOPE. You realize you're my second-in-command now, don't you?

TROTTER. Well, you 'adn't said nothing about it, but——

STANHOPE. Well, you are.

TROTTER. Righto, skipper. (*He pauses*) Thanks. (*He goes towards the steps*) I won't let you down.

STANHOPE. After your duty, have a decent sleep. We must be ready at half-past five.

TROTTER. Righto, skipper. Well, I'll be going up. Give me a chance to cool off up there. It's as 'ot as 'ell in 'ere, with all them damn candles burning.

(*Electrics Cue 1. Go*)

STANHOPE. I suppose it is. My head's nearly splitting. (*He blows out three of the candles, leaving the dim light of one*)

TROTTER (*from top of the steps*) There's a bit of a mist rising.

STANHOPE (*dully*) Is there?

(TROTTER *disappears into the night.*
STANHOPE *broods over his note-book at the table*)

Mason!

MASON (*outside*) Yessir!

STANHOPE. You can bring Mr Raleigh's dinner.

MASON. Very good, sir.

(*Presently* RALEIGH *comes slowly down the steps. He pauses at the bottom, takes off his equipment and places it on the bed* R. MASON *brings in his dinner and puts it on table* R *of Stanhope, and exits.*

STANHOPE *is sitting at the table puffing at the remains of his cigar. There is silence except for the rumble of the guns*)

STANHOPE. I thought I told you to come down to dinner at eight o'clock?

RALEIGH. Oh, I'm sorry. I didn't think you—er——

STANHOPE. Well? You didn't think I—er—what?

RALEIGH. I didn't think you'd—you'd mind—if I didn't.

STANHOPE. I see. And why do you think I asked you—if I didn't mind?

RALEIGH (*by the dug-out door* R) I'm sorry.

STANHOPE. Well, we've kept your dinner. It's ready for you here.

RALEIGH. Oh, it's awfully good of you to have kept it for me, but—I—I had something to eat up there.

STANHOPE. You—had something to eat up there? What do you mean, exactly?

RALEIGH. They brought the tea round while I was on duty. I had a cup, and some bread and cheese.

STANHOPE. Are you telling me—you've been feeding with the men?

RALEIGH. Well, Sergeant Baker suggested——

STANHOPE. So you take your orders from Sergeant Baker, do you?

RALEIGH. No, but——

STANHOPE. You eat the men's rations when there's barely enough for each man?

RALEIGH. They asked me to share.

STANHOPE. Now, look here. I know you're new to this, but I

thought you'd have the common sense to leave the men alone to their meals. Do you think they want an officer prowling round eating their rations, and sucking up to them like that? My officers are here to be respected—not laughed at.

RALEIGH. Why did they ask me—if they didn't mean it?

STANHOPE. Don't you realize they were making a fool of you?

RALEIGH (*quickly*) Why should they?

STANHOPE. So you know more about my men than I do?

(*There is silence.* RALEIGH *is facing Stanhope squarely*)

RALEIGH. I'm sorry then—if I was wrong.

STANHOPE. Sit down.

RALEIGH. It's all right, thanks.

STANHOPE (*suddenly shouting*) Sit down!

(RALEIGH *comes slowly and sits on the box to the right of the table.* STANHOPE *speaks quietly again*)

I understand you prefer being up there with the men than down here with us?

RALEIGH. I don't see what you mean.

STANHOPE. What did you tell Hibbert?

RALEIGH. Hibbert? I—I didn't say——

STANHOPE. Don't lie.

RALEIGH (*rising, knocking over box in doing so, and facing Stanhope squarely*) I'm not lying! Why should I—lie?

STANHOPE. Then why didn't you come down to supper when I told you to?

RALEIGH. I—I wasn't hungry. I had rather a headache. It's cooler up there.

STANHOPE. You insulted Trotter and Hibbert by not coming. You realize that, I suppose?

RALEIGH. I didn't mean to do anything like that.

STANHOPE. Well, you did. You know now—don't you?

(RALEIGH *makes no reply. He is trying to understand why Stanhope's temper has risen to a trembling fury.* STANHOPE *can scarcely control his voice*)

(*Loudly*) I say—you *know* now, don't you?

RALEIGH. Yes, I'm sorry.

STANHOPE. My officers work *together*. I'll have no damn prigs.

RALEIGH (*looking hard at Stanhope*). I'll speak to Trotter and Hibbert. I didn't realize——

(STANHOPE *raises his cigar. His hand trembles so violently that he can scarcely take the cigar between his teeth.* RALEIGH *looks at Stanhope, fascinated and horrified*)

STANHOPE. I'm glad you didn't realize—— What are you looking at?

RALEIGH (*lowering his head*) Nothing.

STANHOPE. Anything—*funny* about me?

RALEIGH. No.

(*After a moment's silence,* RALEIGH *speaks in a low, halting voice. He drops his head, finds this difficult to say*)

I'm awfully sorry, Dennis, if—if I annoyed you by coming to your company.

STANHOPE. What on *earth* are you talking about? What do you mean?

RALEIGH. You resent my being here.

STANHOPE. Resent you *being* here?

RALEIGH. Ever since I came——

STANHOPE. I don't know what you mean. I resent you being a damn fool, that's all. (*There is a pause*) Better eat your dinner before it's cold.

RALEIGH. I'm not hungry, thanks.

STANHOPE. Oh, for God's sake, sit down and eat it like a man!

RALEIGH. I can't eat it, thanks.

STANHOPE (*shouting*) Are you going to eat your dinner?

RALEIGH. Good God! Don't you understand? How *can* I sit down and eat that—when—(*his voice is nearly breaking*)—when Osborne's—lying—out there—— (*He points out to the trenches*)

(STANHOPE, *rising and leaning against post for support, his eyes are wide and staring; he is fighting for breath, and his words come brokenly*)

STANHOPE. My God! You bloody little swine! You think I don't care—you think you're the only soul that cares.

RALEIGH. And yet you can sit there and drink champagne—and smoke cigars——

STANHOPE. The one man I could trust—my best friend—the one man I could talk to as man to man—who understood every-thing—and you think I don't care——

RALEIGH. But how can you when——?

STANHOPE. To forget, you little fool—to forget! D'you under-stand? To forget! You think there's no limit to what a man can bear?

(*He turns quickly from Raleigh and goes to the dark corner up* R. *He stands with his face towards the wall, his shoulders heaving as he fights for breath, sobbing bitterly*)

RALEIGH (*turning to him and speaking very quietly*) I'm awfully sorry, Dennis. I—I didn't understand.

(*Stanhope makes no reply*)

You don't know how—I——

STANHOPE. Go away, please—leave me alone.

RALEIGH. Can't I——

(STANHOPE *turns wildly upon Raleigh*)

STANHOPE. Oh, get out. For God's sake, get out!

(RALEIGH *goes towards his dug-out, turns again and slowly goes out* R, *and Stanhope is alone. After Raleigh has gone* STANHOPE *continues to sob. Gropes for the bed and falls on his knees into it. His heart is breaking. The 'Verey' lights rise and fall outside, softly breaking the darkness with their glow—sometimes steel-blue, sometimes grey. Through the night there comes the impatient grumble of gunfire that never dies away*)

The CURTAIN *falls*

SCENE 3

The SCENE *opens in complete darkness.*

Towards dawn. The candles are no longer burning. The intense darkness of the dug-out is softened by the glow of the 'Verey' lights in the sky beyond the doorway. There is no sound except the distant mutter of the guns.

A runner is asleep on the steps.

As the CURTAIN *rises* MASON *comes from the servant's dug-out; for a moment his head and shoulders stand out black against the glowing sky; he sleepily staggers up to the runner and shakes him, asking the time. There is no reply. He returns to the table, knocks into a box, and says 'Damn'. There comes the rasp of a striking match (Electrics Cue 1. Go.)—a tiny flame—and a candle gleams. MASON blinks in the light and turns to Stanhope's bed. STANHOPE lies huddled with his blanket drawn tightly round him.*

MASON (*softly*) Sir——

(STANHOPE *does not move;* MASON *shakes him gently by the knee*)

(*A little louder*) Sir——

STANHOPE. Yes? (*There is a pause*) That you, Mason?

MASON. 'Arf-past five, sir.

STANHOPE. Oh, right. (*He sits up, shakes himself, raises himself on his elbow*) I was only half asleep. I keep on waking up. It's so frightfully cold in here.

MASON. It's a cold dug-out, this one, sir. I've made some 'ot tea.

STANHOPE. Good. You might bring me some.

MASON. Right you are, sir.

STANHOPE. And take some to the officers in there—and wake them up.

MASON. Very good, sir.

(MASON *exits to his dug-out up* L.)

STANHOPE *rises stiffly from his bed, shudders from the cold, and slowly begins putting his equipment on.*

TROTTER *wanders in from his dug-out vigorously lathering his face. He is dressed, except for his collar)*

TROTTER. Wash and brush-up, tuppence!

STANHOPE (*looking up, surprised*) Hullo! I thought you were asleep.

TROTTER. I 'ad a decent sleep when I come off dooty. What's the time?

STANHOPE. Half-past five. It'll be getting light soon. You better buck up.

TROTTER. All right. *I* shan't be long. Sounds quiet enough out there.

STANHOPE. Yes.

(MASON *brings four mugs of tea)*

TROTTER. Ah! that's what I want. A decent cup of tea.

MASON (*putting a mug on the table for Stanhope*) Nice and 'ot, sir. I've cut a packet of sambridges for each gentleman, sir.

STANHOPE. Good.

(MASON *takes the other mugs of tea into the* R *dug-out.* TROTTER *is following, lathering with gusto)*

You might give Hibbert and Raleigh a call.

TROTTER. I woke 'em up, skipper. They're getting their things on.

(*He exits into the dug-out.*
    MASON *returns)*

STANHOPE. When you've cleaned up your kitchen, you must dress and join your platoon in the line.

MASON. Very good, sir.

STANHOPE. If things are going well at eleven o'clock, come down here and do your best to get some lunch for us. We shall come down in turn as we can.

MASON. Very good, sir.

(STANHOPE *sits at the table and begins to write a short report. The first sign of dawn is beginning to gleam in the dark sky.* STANHOPE *calls* 'Runner!' *as he writes. A* SOLDIER *comes down the steps and stands at attention* RC)

STANHOPE (*folding the note*) Take this to Battalion Head-quarters. There's no reply.

SOLDIER. Yessir.

(*The* SOLDIER *salutes and exits up the steps.*
    L STANHOPE *resumes his writing. A plaintive noise comes from the other dug-out.* TROTTER *is singing* 'There's a long, long trail

a-winding'. Stanhope *listens for a moment, then rises, takes a few small coins from his pocket, and throws them into Trotter's dug-out. The singing stops abruptly. After a moment* Trotter's *voice comes*)

Trotter. Thank you kindly, gov'nor!

(*The* Sergeant-Major *comes down the steps and stands* RC. *Electrics Cue* 2)

Stanhope. Morning, Sergeant-Major.

Sergeant-Major. Morning, sir. Wiring parties are just in, sir. Made a decent job of it—right down to the support line.

Stanhope. Good. Everything quiet?

Sergeant-Major. It's all right opposite 'ere, sir, but the guns are goin' 'ard down south. 'Eavy bombardment. Not sure if it ain't spreading up this way, sir.

Stanhope. Very likely it is. The officers are coming up in a minute. They'll stand by with their platoons. I must stay here awhile in case of messages. I shall come up directly things begin to happen.

Sergeant-Major. Very good, sir.

Stanhope. Are the men having their tea?

Sergeant-Major. Yessir.

Stanhope. Let 'em have a decent drop of rum.

Sergeant-Major. About 'arf again, sir?

Stanhope. Yes.

Sergeant-Major. If the attack don't come, sir, 'ow long are we to stand-to?

Stanhope. We must expect the attack any time up till midday. After then I don't think it'll come till tomorrow.

Sergeant-Major. Very good, sir.

Stanhope. We must naturally make our plans to meet things as they happen.

Sergeant-Major. Quite, sir.

Stanhope. All right, Sergeant-Major. I'll see you up there soon.

Sergeant-Major. Yessir. (*He salutes and goes away*)

(Mason *brings in four little packets of sandwiches, and puts one packet on the table for Stanhope. Moves to* RC)

Mason. Your sambridges, sir. 'Arf bully beef and 'arf sardine. Sardine on top, sir.

Stanhope. How delicious. No *pâté de foie gras*?

Mason. No what, sir?

Stanhope. No *pâté de foie gras*?

Mason. No, sir. The milkman 'asn't been yet.

(Mason *takes the other parcels to the* R *dug-out.* Stanhope *pours a little whiskey into his tea and the remainder of the contents of the bottle into his flask.* Mason *returns*)

STANHOPE. Get dressed as soon as you can.
MASON. Yessir.

(MASON *goes out up* L.
TROTTER comes in, fully dressed for the line)

TROTTER. All ready, skipper. Want me to go up?
STANHOPE. Yes. I think so. Go right round the line and see everything's all right. I'll be up soon.

(*First bang—medium.*
Suddenly there comes the faint whistle and thud of falling shells—a few seconds between each. STANHOPE *and* TROTTER *listen intently, four shells fall, then silence.*
Second bang—medium)

TROTTER. 'Ullo, 'ullo.

(STANHOPE *strides to the doorway, goes up a few steps, and looks out into the night. He comes slowly back*)

STANHOPE. Over on Lancer's Alley—somewhere by the reserve line.

(*Third bang—loud.*
There comes the louder thud of three more shells)

TROTTER. That's nearer.
STANHOPE. Better go up, Trotter. Call the others.
TROTTER (*at the* R *dug-out*) 'Ibbert! Raleigh! come on! (*He crosses to the table and lights a cigarette over the candle, lingers a moment, and slowly goes up the steps*) Cheero, skipper. See you later.
STANHOPE. Send your runner down to tell me how things are going.
TROTTER. Righto.

(TROTTER *disappears into the dark. A vague white line of dawn is broadening above the dark trench wall outside.* STANHOPE *sits at the table and sips his tea. He takes a cigarette and lights it with a quivering hand.* RALEIGH *comes from his dug-out.* STANHOPE *lowers his head and writes in his note-book*)

RALEIGH. Do you want me to go up?
STANHOPE (*without looking up*) Yes. Trotter's gone.
RALEIGH. Right. (*He goes up the steps and on the top step turns and says shyly*) Cheero—Stanhope.
STANHOPE (*still writing with lowered head*) Cheero, Raleigh. I shall be coming up soon.

(RALEIGH *goes up the steps and exits.*
STANHOPE *stops writing, raises his head, and listens. The shells are falling steadily now. He glances towards the* R *dug-out and calls:*)

Hibbert!

(*There is no reply. He slowly rises and goes to the* R *dug-out doorway. He calls again—louder:*)

Hibbert!! (*He looks into the doorway and says*) What are you doing?

(HIBBERT *appears. He is very pale; he moves as if half asleep*)

Come along, man!

HIBBERT. You want me to go up now? (*He moves over to* L)

STANHOPE. Of course I do. The others have gone.

HIBBERT. Got a drop of water?

STANHOPE. What d'you want water for?

HIBBERT. I'm so frightfully thirsty. All that champagne and stuff—dried my mouth up.

(STANHOPE *pours out a drink into a mug and gives it to Hibbert*)

STANHOPE. Here you are. Didn't you have any tea?

HIBBERT. Yes. It was a bit sweet, though.

(*The shelling is steadily increasing, and now, above the lighter 'crush' of the smaller shells, there comes the deep, resounding 'boom' of Minenwerfer.* HIBBERT *sips his water very slowly, rinsing his mouth deliberately with each sip.* STANHOPE *is by the doorway, looking up into the trench. He has just turned away as a sonorous drawn-out call comes floating through the dawn:* 'Stretcher bearers!' STANHOPE *half turns, then faces Hibbert*)

STANHOPE. Come on. Buck up.

HIBBERT. There's no appalling hurry, is there?

STANHOPE. No hurry! Why d'you think the others have gone up?

HIBBERT (*slowly*) What? Trotter and Raleigh?

STANHOPE (*sharply*) Wake up, man! What the devil's the matter with you?

(HIBBERT *slowly puts down his mug*)

HIBBERT. Champagne dries the mouth up so. Makes the tongue feel like a bit of paper.

(*There is a slight pause*)

STANHOPE. The longer you stay here, the harder it'll be to go up.

HIBBERT. Good Lord! You don't think I'm——

STANHOPE. You're just wasting as much time as you can.

HIBBERT. Well, damn it, it's no good going up till I feel fit. Let's just have another spot of water.

(HIBBERT *takes the jug and pours out a little more water. He is the picture of misery.* STANHOPE *stands impatiently beside him. Stanhope is* RC. *Hibbert* L. MASON *appears from his dug-out, fully dressed for the line, his rifle slung over his shoulder*)

Mason (l *of* c) I'll go right along, sir. I've made up the fire to last a good three hours—if you don't mind me popping down about nine o'clock to 'ave a look at it.

Stanhope. All right, Mason. Mr Hibbert's coming up now. You can go along with him.

Mason (*to Hibbert*) I'd like to come along of you if you don't mind, sir. I ain't bin up in this part of the front line. Don't want to get lorst.

Stanhope. Mr Hibbert'll show you the way up. (*He turns to Hibbert*) Keep your men against the back wall of the trench as long as the shells are dropping behind. Cheero!

(Hibbert *looks at Stanhope for a moment, then, with a slight smile, he goes slowly up the steps and into the trench,* Mason *following behind.*

A dark figure stands out against the pale sky; the runner comes hurrying down the steps, out of breath and excited, standing rc)

Yes?

Soldier. Message from Mr Trotter, sir. Shells falling mostly behind support line. Minnies along front line.

Stanhope. Who's just been hit?

Soldier. Corporal Ross, I think it was, sir. Minnie dropped in the trench at the corner—just as I come away.

(*The* Sergeant-Major *comes down the steps, very much out of breath*)

Stanhope (*to the Soldier*) All right, thanks.

(*The* Soldier *salutes, and goes up the steps slower than he came*)

Sergeant-Major. Beginning to get 'ot, sir.

Stanhope. Corporal Ross hit?

Sergeant-Major. Yessir.

Stanhope. Badly?

Sergeant-Major. Pretty badly, sir.

Stanhope. Most of the shelling's going over, isn't it?

Sergeant-Major. Most of the *shells* is be'ind, sir, but there's Minnies and rifle grenades along the front line. Pretty 'ot it's getting, sir. They're attacking down south—there's rifle fire.

Stanhope. All right, Sergeant-Major; thanks.

Sergeant-Major. What I come to ask, sir—what about the wounded—getting 'em down, sir? The shelling's pretty thick over Lancer's Alley.

Stanhope. What about Fosse Way?

Sergeant-Major. Pretty bad there, too, sir.

Stanhope. Don't try then. Take anyone badly hit down into the big dug-out on the right. Let the stretcher bearers do what they can there.

Sergeant-Major. Very good, sir.

STANHOPE. Only Corporal Ross hit?

SERGEANT-MAJOR. That's all, sir——

(*Again there comes the drawn-out call—several times as it is passed from man to man:* 'Stretcher bear-ers!'
The falling of shells increases here.
The SERGEANT-MAJOR'S *eyes meet* STANHOPE'S. *He turns and goes up the steps quickly. Stanhope is alone. Flying fragments of shell whistle and hiss and moan overhead. The sharp 'crack' of the rifle grenades, the thud of the shells, and the boom of the Minenwerfer mingle together in a muffled roar.* STANHOPE *takes his belt from the table and buckles it on, puts his revolver lanyard round his neck, and drops his flask and sandwiches into his pocket, and is putting his papers together. The* SERGEANT-MAJOR *reappears and comes hurrying down the steps very out of breath*)

STANHOPE (*turning quickly*) What is it, Sergeant-Major?

SERGEANT-MAJOR. Mr Raleigh, sir——

STANHOPE. What!

SERGEANT-MAJOR. Mr Raleigh's been 'it, sir. Bit of shell's got 'im in the back.

STANHOPE. Badly?

SERGEANT-MAJOR. 'Fraid it's broke 'is spine, sir; can't move 'is legs.

STANHOPE. Bring him down here.

SERGEANT-MAJOR. Down 'ere, sir?

STANHOPE (*shouting, rapping it out*) Yes! Down here—quickly!

(*The* SERGEANT-MAJOR *hurries up the steps. A shell screams and bursts very near. The* SERGEANT-MAJOR *shrinks back and throws his hand across his face, as though a human hand could ward off the hot flying pieces. He stumbles on again into the trench, and hurriedly away.* STANHOPE *pushes the table up slightly, now starts to arrange the bed* L, *fumbling a blanket over it. He takes a trench coat off the wall and rolls it for a pillow, and turns as the* SERGEANT-MAJOR *comes carefully down the steps carrying* RALEIGH *like a child in his huge arms*)

(*With blanket ready*) Lay him down there.

SERGEANT-MAJOR. 'E's fainted, sir. 'E was conscious when I picked 'im up.

(*The* SERGEANT-MAJOR *lays the boy gently on the bed; he draws away his hands, looks furtively at the palms, and wipes the blood on the sides of his trousers.* STANHOPE *covers Raleigh with his blanket, looks intently at the boy, and turns to the* SERGEANT-MAJOR, *who has moved slightly up* C)

STANHOPE. Have they dressed the wound?

SERGEANT-MAJOR. They've just put a pad on it, sir. Can't do no more.

STANHOPE. Go at once and bring two men with a stretcher.

SERGEANT-MAJOR. We'll never get 'im down, sir, with them shells falling on Lancer's Alley.

STANHOPE (*rapping this out again*) Did you hear what I said? Go and get two men with a stretcher.

SERGEANT-MAJOR (*after a moment's hesitation*) Very good, sir.

(*The* SERGEANT-MAJOR *exits slowly.*

STANHOPE *turns to Raleigh once more, then goes to the table, pushes his handkerchief into the water-jug, and brings it, wringing wet, to Raleigh's bed. He bathes the boy's face. Presently* RALEIGH *gives a little moan, opens his eyes, and turns his head*)

RALEIGH. Hullo—Dennis——

STANHOPE. Well, Jimmy—(*he smiles*)—you got one quickly.

(*There is silence for a while.* STANHOPE *is sitting on a box beside Raleigh. Presently* RALEIGH *speaks again—in a wondering voice*)

RALEIGH. Why—how did I get down here?

STANHOPE. Sergeant-Major brought you down.

(RALEIGH *speaks again, vaguely, trying to recollect*)

RALEIGH. Something—hit me in the back—knocked me clean over—sort of—winded me—— I'm all right now. (*He tries to rise*)

STANHOPE. Steady, old boy. Just lie there quietly for a bit.

RALEIGH. I'll be better if I get up and walk about. It happened once before—I got kicked in just the same place at Rugger; it—it soon wore off. It—it just numbs you for a bit. (*There is a pause*) What's that rumbling noise?

STANHOPE. The guns are making a bit of a row.

RALEIGH. Our guns?

STANHOPE. No. Mostly theirs.

(*Again there is silence in the dug-out. A very faint rose light is beginning to glow in the dawn sky.* RALEIGH *speaks again—uneasily*)

RALEIGH. I say—Dennis——

STANHOPE. Yes, old boy?

RALEIGH. It—it hasn't gone through, has it? It only just hit me? —and knocked me down?

STANHOPE. It's just gone through a bit, Jimmy.

RALEIGH. I won't have to—go on lying here?

STANHOPE. I'm going to have you taken away.

RALEIGH. Away? Where?

STANHOPE. Down to the dressing-station—then hospital—then home. (*He smiles*) You've got a Blighty one, Jimmy.

RALEIGH. But I—I can't go home just for—for a knock in the back. (*He stirs restlessly*) I'm certain I'll be better if—if I get up. (*He tries to raise himself, and gives a sudden cry*) Oh—God! It does hurt!

STANHOPE. It's bound to hurt, Jimmy.

RALEIGH. What's—on my legs? Something holding them down——
STANHOPE. It's all right, old chap; it's just the shock—numbed them.

(*Again there is a pause. When* RALEIGH *speaks, there is a different note in his voice*)

RALEIGH. It's awfully decent of you to bother, Dennis. I feel rotten lying here—everybody else—up there.
STANHOPE. It's not your fault, Jimmy.
RALEIGH. So—damn—silly—getting hit. (*Pause*) Is there—just a drop of water?
STANHOPE (*rising quickly*) Sure. I've got some here.

(*He pours some water into the mug, rinses it out, re-fills it and raises* RALEIGH'S *head as he gives him a drink*)

(*Cheerfully*) Got some tea-leaves in it. D'you mind?
RALEIGH. No. That's all right—thanks——

(STANHOPE *holds the mug to* RALEIGH'S *lips, and the boy drinks*)

I say, Dennis, don't you wait—if—if you want to be getting on.
STANHOPE. It's quite all right, Jimmy.
RALEIGH. Can you stay for a bit?
STANHOPE. Of course I can.
RALEIGH (*faintly*) Thanks awfully.

(*There is quiet in the dug-out for a time.* STANHOPE *sits with one hand on Raleigh's arm, and* RALEIGH *lies very still. Presently he speaks again—hardly above a whisper*)

Dennis——
STANHOPE. Yes, old boy?
RALEIGH. Could we have a light? It's—it's so frightfully dark and cold.
STANHOPE (*rising*) Sure! I'll bring a candle and get another blanket.

(STANHOPE *goes out* R, *and* RALEIGH *is alone, very still and quiet. The faint rosy glow of the dawn is deepening to an angry red. The grey night sky is dissolving, and the stars begin to go. A tiny sound comes from where* RALEIGH *is lying—something between a sob and a moan, his* L *hand drops to the floor.* STANHOPE *comes back with a blanket. He takes a candle from the table and carries it to Raleigh's bed. He puts it on the box beside Raleigh and speaks cheerfully*)

Is that better, Jimmy? (RALEIGH *makes no sign*) Jimmy——

(*Still* RALEIGH *is quiet.* STANHOPE *gently takes his hand. There is a long silence.* STANHOPE *lowers Raleigh's hand to the bed. The solitary candle-flame throws up the lines on his pale, drawn face, and the dark shadows under his tired eyes. The thudding of the shells rises and falls like an angry sea.*

The RUNNER *comes scrambling down the steps, his round, red face wet with perspiration, his chest heaving for breath, and looks at Stanhope the whole time)*

SOLDIER. Message from Mr Trotter, sir—will you come at once.

(STANHOPE *gazes round at the Soldier—and makes no other sign*)

Mr Trotter, sir—says will you come at once!

(STANHOPE *rises stiffly and takes his tin hat off the wall*)

STANHOPE. All right, Broughton, I'm coming.

(*The* SOLDIER *turns and goes quickly up the steps.*

STANHOPE *pauses for a moment by the bed, and, as he moves away, he lightly runs his fingers over Raleigh's tousled hair. Very slowly he walks to the bottom of the steps. As he gets there he stops for a second and then he goes stiffly up the steps, his tall figure black against the dawn sky as he exits.*

Electrics Cue 3.

The shelling has risen to a great fury. The solitary candle burns with a steady flame, and RALEIGH *lies in the shadows. The whine of a shell rises to a shriek and bursts on the dug-out roof. The shock stabs out the candle-flame; the timber props of the door cave slowly in, sand-bags fall and block the passage to the open air. There is darkness in the dug-out. Here and there the red dawn glows through the jagged holes of the broken doorway. Very faintly there comes the dull rattle of machine-guns and the fevered spatter of rifle fire.*

The lights fade out)

CURTAIN

A, B, C, D, shorings for roof, B and C to fall at end of play. Dotted lines and arrow mark position of ceiling.

PROPERTY PLOT

ACT I

Hanging on Nails round interior of Scene:

Over Bed.— Coat, 2 ammunition belts, water-bottle, trench tool-bag, haversack.

Over Opening L.—3 packs, 1 trench hat.

On Wall, back.—2 coats, 3 gas masks, 2 hats, 2 packs, ammunition belt, red blanket rolled up over opening.

On Wall L.— 1 gas-mask case, trench tool-bag, cuttings and illustrations from magazines and *La Vie Parisienne.*

On Post L.— Pack, old sack.

On Post C.—Ammunition-case, water-bottle, post-card photo.

On Post R.—Gas-mask case, bunch of notes.

On Steps C.—Pieces of old sacks, and dirt.

On Rostrum at back.—3 packs, ammunition-belt, water-bottle, trench tool-bag, 2 gas-mask cases.

Rubbish and quantity of old papers scattered over floor and under beds. Pieces of dirty sacking and canvas thrown in corners and hanging round scene.

(All the above Properties are dressing and not moved)

On Backing L.—Coat and pack.

On Backing R.—Gas-mask case.

Candle alight (only put out at opening of Act III, Scene 3, and Finale).

Wire-netting bed against wall R.

Wire-netting bed against wall L.

Brown blanket on each bed.

Pack (for pillow) on bed L.

Rough form at back L, with hat and gas-mask case.

Rough table in front of posts L.

Dirty box above table.

Dirty box R of table.

Narrow oblong box in front of table (for awkward seat).

Dirty rag on box in front of table.

Log book hung over bed L.

Canvas bucket of water down stage R.

On Table.—2 maps, tin of cigarettes.

Small rum jar, water, whiskey bottle with small quantity of whiskey, 3 enamel mugs.

2 fruit tins with lit candles.

Under Table.—Dirty cigar box with 3 candles, and dirty list of stores.

HARDY's equipment on bed R.

HARDY's walking-stick on post R.

Off Stage R.—Bass drum and iron tank (for distant rumble of gun-fire).

Shot-pad and beaters (maxim-gun).

Syren, pad and heavy beater (shell-fire).

Off Stage L.—MASON properties (order of going on):

2 double pages of newspaper (tablecloth).

4 knives, 4 forks, 4 spoons.

Plate of (dog) biscuits.

2 plates of soup, bottle of whiskey (full), 2 mugs (small).

2 plates of soup.

Frying-pan, 4 cutlets (ginger-bread), fork.

1 large mug and 3 small mugs of coffee on plate.

Blanket.

Personal Properties

RALEIGH.—Walking-stick, pipe, tobacco in pouch.
OSBORNE.—Pipe, tobacco-pouch and tobacco, cigarettes in case, watch on strap, ring, note-book (Army book 153), pencil.
STANHOPE.—Army note-book and pencil, small pocket wallet with photo of girl.
TROTTER.—Small stub pencil.

PERISHABLE PROPERTIES REQUIRED

Bovril (for soup), bacon, bread, milk, coffee, tea, bananas (bacon), sardines, butter, tobacco, cigarettes, cigars, dry ginger ale (champagne), candles, matches, ginger-bread (cutlets), dog biscuits (Army biscuits).
Lunch biscuits (used with dog biscuits for TROTTER to eat).
Burnt sugar (whiskey colouring).
Notepaper and envelopes (for letters).
Strawberry jam.
Newspaper (English, large size, for tablecloth)—*Morning Post* or *Telegraph.*
Small bar of chocolate and few sweets (GERMAN PRISONER).
Shaving-cream.
Smoke-bombs.
Fuller's earth.
Cartridges.

Properties on Table (discovered)

Tin of cigarettes.
Rum jar.
Whiskey bottle (small amount in same).
3 enamel mugs.
2 candle tins with lighted candles.

ACT II

SCENE 1

Properties on Table (discovered)

Newspaper tablecloth.
Tin of cigarettes.
2 candles (lighted) in tins.
Magazine, biscuit under same.
3 knives and forks.
2 mugs of coffee.
2 plates of bacon.
Plate of biscuits.
Tin of strawberry jam and spoon.
2 maps.
La Vie Parisienne (on bed L).
Rum jar (on floor by table).
Drum, tank, syren and shot-pads (*off stage* R).
Off Stage L, *for* MASON.—Knife, fork, spoon, mug of coffee, plate of porridge (milk), drying-pan, bacon, fork and plate, plate of sardines, mug of tea, bottle of whiskey, 2 mugs.

Personal Properties

COLONEL.—Walking-stick.

SCENE 2

Larger box in front of table.
On Table.—2 maps, bottle of whiskey, 3 mugs, tin of cigarettes.

Off Stage R.—Drum and tank (rumbles only).
Off Stage L, *for* MASON.—2 large mugs of coffee, tin of jam and spoon, mug of coffee, plate of bread and butter, mug of coffee.

Personal Properties

SERGEANT-MAJOR.—Small note-book and pencil.
OSBORNE.—Book (*Alice in Wonderland*), note-book and pencil.

ACT III

SCENE 1

On Table.—2 candles in tins, 2 maps, 3 mugs, bottle of whiskey.
Off Stage R.—Drum and tank.
  Raid effects, shot-pad and beater (maxim-gun).
  2 small cannon.
  3 revolvers fully loaded.
  Smoke-screen effect behind rostrum.
  Small fall of earth at entrance C during raid.
Off Stage L, *for* MASON.—2 large mugs of coffee, dishcloth.

Personal Properties

OSBORNE.—Ring, watch, letter (addressed to Mrs Osborne), old letters and papers, pipe and tobacco, case of cigarettes.
RALEIGH.—Letters.
GERMAN PRISONER.—Paybook, bundle of letters, piece of string, small paper bag of sweets, small bar of chocolate, pocket-knife, pencil.

SCENE 2

On Table.—Newspaper tablecloth, remains of dinner for three, 2 bottles of champagne (half full), 5 candles burning in tins, 3 cigars, 4 mugs.
Off R.—Drum and tank (rumbles).
Off L.—Full bottle of whiskey, 2 mugs, 1 large mug of coffee, plate of food (hot—not eaten), knife and fork.

Personal Properties

HIBBERT.—4 vulgar post-cards.

SCENE 3

On Table.—Cigarettes in tin, 1 candle in tin (not lit), 2 mugs, map, rum jar and bottle of whiskey.
  Note-book and pencil (for STANHOPE).
  STANHOPE's hat hung downstage over bed.
  Boxes pushed close to table, except box behind table.
  Blanket from bed R on form at back.
Off Stage R.—Drum, tank, shot-pad, syren and shot-pad (shell fire), 1 revolver shot for third shell effect.
  TROTTER.—Shaving soap, hot water and shaving-brush.
Off Stage L.—Stretcher.
  For MASON, box of matches, 4 parcels of sandwiches (small), 4 small mugs of coffee on a plate, blanket.
  For STANHOPE.—Blanket and lighted candles in tin with reflector to throw light upon face, flash and khaki handkerchief.

Note for Property Master at finish of play

When final explosion goes from the electric 3 maroons, the 2 yacht cannons are let off together. The peat box above the door drops first. A pause, then the four beams.

Electrics Cue 4. Go
Then CURTAIN

ELECTRICAL PLOT

Position of Lamps—
    No. 1—Spot on O.P. (R) end of table.
    No. 2—Spot up stage C of table.
    No. 3—Spot prompt (L) end of table.
    No. 4—Spot to take in C of table (spare—*only used in emergency*).
    No. 5—Spot to take in C of table.

ACT I

To Open.—Portable board—1, 2, 3 and 5 up to mark.
    Floats.—Baby spot, FULL.
    Stage—Prompt Side (L)—Flood (double blue), FULL.
    At Cue.—When OSBORNE blows candle out—1, 2, 3 and 5 spots down half.
During the First Act the 'Verey' light comes on and off every minute through-
    out the Act.

ACT II

SCENE 1

To Open.—Portable board—1, 2, 3 and 5 up to mark.
    Floats.—Baby spot, FULL.
    Stage.—Prompt side (L).—Flood (*amber*) up to mark.
        O.P. (R).—Amber up to mark.
    No. 6 Batten.—One circuit white.
At Cue: 'You can see the bit of lean quite clear.'—Start Sun.

SCENE 2
Same, but no sun.

ACT III

SCENE 1

To Open.—Portable board—1, 2, 3 up to mark.
    Floats.—Baby spot, FULL.
    Stage.—Prompt (L).—Flood (*double blue*), FULL.
        O.P. (R)—Flood (amber) up to mark.
    Batten No. 6.—Three-circuit white.
At Cue: 'The time has come, the Walrus said.'—Check batten 6 and O.P.
    Flood (R). Both to be out at end of raid.

SCENE 2

Portable Board.—Same.
Floats.—Same.
Stage.—Blue spot on backcloth.
At Cue: 'Hot as Hell.'—Check spots 1, 2, 3 up to mark. 'Verey' light through-
    out this scene.

SCENE 3

To Open.—Black Out.
At Cue: Lighting of candle.—1, 2, 3 up to mark.
Floats.—Baby spot, FULL.
At Cue: 'Take this to Battalion Headquarters.'—Bring in O.P. (R) flood amber
    up to mark. Then red spot on backcloth slowly up to mark.
At Cue: Final shell. Black Out. 'Verey' light throughout.

REQUIREMENTS

On 1st set of lines behind Act Drop.—Iron channel barrel to take 5 spots.
5 500-watt spot lamps for same.
Baby float spot.
Above Trench Rostrum.—10-foot iron barrel to take 3 spots: 2 on backcloth, 1 for sunlight into trench.
On Stage.—1 500-watt flood, slung on line for 'Verey' light.
2 500-watt flood lamps on high stands to light backcloth, 1 R and 1 L.
3 flash-boxes.
Switchboard for maroons (fired electrically).
NOTE.—No floats.
Keep house batten over trench rostrum alive (*one circuit white*).

MADE AND PRINTED IN GREAT BRITAIN BY
LATIMER TREND & COMPANY LTD PLYMOUTH
MADE IN ENGLAND